How to Stop Procrastinating & Start Living

Lore
Broa

AUGSBURG Publishing House • Minneapolis

HOW TO STOP PROCRASTINATING
AND START LIVING

MANUFACTURED IN THE UNITED STATES OF AMERICA

To Catherine,
the most interesting, entertaining, insightful,
and intimate person I've ever known

Contents

Preface

This book is written for:

- people who procrastinate and want to eliminate the habit,
- the families of procrastinators suffering because of the habit,
- employers frustrated with so many missed deadlines by employees,
- employees inconvenienced by procrastinating bosses,
- parents who want to help their children avoid this harmful habit,
- teachers who want to help students develop a more responsible way of living,
- Christians who want to decrease apathy, eliminate unnecessary conflict, and live their faith more joyously.

Procrastination is more than a simple habit; it is a way of life for many people—an attitude toward work, play, and others. People who procrastinate can be classified into two broad categories.

The first consists of people who procrastinate because they lack skills; they do not know how to organize their time and set priorities. This book describes methods for developing these skills, and if you use the skills and principles suggested, you will overcome the troublesome habit of postponing what you think and feel ought to be done.

The problem with this solution is that resolving the problem is not that easy, as every procrastinator knows. Few people are helped simply by knowing how to organize their time and set priorities. However, after one understands the causes of procrastination and practices the cures suggested, time-management and organizational principles will aid in managing tasks joyously.

The second category consists of people who procrastinate because complex motivational forces block their good intentions. This book describes the problems created by procrastination, examines the causes, and suggests several methods for curing the "disease." Anyone determined to develop a new attitude toward work, play, and people will find the resources necessary for that change.

Discovering the causes and cures for procrastination has been a fascinating experience for one who has been confused by it for more than 20 years. First, I fought the battle within myself and, at times, still fight it. Second, I have observed others enslaved by the paralyzing problem from several professional positions: sales manager of Foremost International Dairies, Director of Development for Lexington Theological Seminary, minister of three congregations, and professor at Lexington Theological Seminary with the responsibility for teaching people "how to get the job done."

Hundreds of people participated in the research for this book through interviews, questionnaires, letters, and group discussions. I have tested the cures for procrastination with individuals and in groups. After the cures were tested, they were used in scores of seminars for people from all segments of society—private business, professional organizations, and governmental, educational, and religious agencies. I appreciate each person's help in un-

8

derstanding the causes and cures of procrastination. Some names and minor details of incidents described in the book have been changed to protect the identity of those involved.

Lexington Theological Seminary's generous sabbatical program enabled me to research procrastination and to write this book. For their support in this project I thank the trustees, administrative officers, faculty members, and staff of Lexington Theological Seminary.

Ellis Yonge, my father-in-law, latched onto this subject with the dedication of a new father teaching his son to walk; a steady stream of insights from Ellis sailed through the mail during the research. I owe him more than print can express.

James M. Wray Jr. criticized the manuscript in its early stages. Augsburg editors guided the development of the book to its final form. I appreciate the help of these skilled professionals.

Mary Cole and Nan McSwain typed the manuscript and Carole Davis typed correspondence to the editors. I appreciate working with these patient, pleasant persons.

Part One

Procrastination & the Procrastinator

1

Are You a Procrastinator?

I am a fumbling fix-it man. For some unknown reason, caulking the tub does not thrill me, and a leaky faucet is my cross to bear. When the faucet starts leaking and I reach for the pipe wrench, I know that my sense of self-worth is going to be bruised as well as my knuckles. For when I get the top off the dripless faucet (the company makes a repair kit for fixing the dripless faucet when it starts dripping), I will be confused, then skinned, and finally angry. During this confrontation with the inanimate object I exhaust my vocabulary to no avail; the faucet still drips. So I postpone as long as possible the humiliating encounter.

In 1974 a FOR SALE sign appeared in the front yard of our neighbor's house. My wife commented, "Where else can you buy a house in July with Christmas lights already strung up around the eaves?"

Because he was three months overdue with his weekly sales report, a super salesman prompted his company to establish a policy that no one gets paid until all sales reports are completed and submitted to the office.

Each year George says he will figure his income tax early, but each year he postpones it until the week before it's due. Because he doesn't get all his records for the past year together on time, he can't take all the deductions to which he is entitled. Therefore he ends up paying more taxes than he should.

While attending a five-day seminar in Nashville, ten of us decided to break the monotony by dining out. During the first three days of the seminar I suppressed my desire to talk about procrastination, but this evening was perfect for a little research. I waited for an opening. During the salad course someone asked, "Loren, how many children do you have?"

"Three," I replied, "and I'm researching procrastination. Some fascinating things about the habit have emerged."

All forks stopped in midair. Mrs. Jones, seated to my right and across the table, almost knocked her husband out of his chair when she lunged in my direction. "What have you learned? He's the worst in the world," she said, pointing to her husband. "I have to push him constantly to get him to do his work. If it weren't for me, we'd be on welfare right now."

Procrastination can cause constant bickering in a family and change a happy marriage into a harrowing battlefield. It freezes bright, talented people in jobs where they become paper pushers doing dull routine work. It causes many to live frustrated, joyless, anxious lives, devoid of the good feeling of accomplishment.

Procrastination is a strange disease. The president of a successful advertising agency may manage the business with the efficiency of a computer, yet cannot get around to having antifreeze put in her car until the temperature plunges to 15 degrees. The minister of a 1000-member congregation may never be late to a meeting or appoint-

14

ment and may finish writing Sunday's sermon on Friday, yet can't seem to answer the mail until it is embarrassing to do so. Some people procrastinate on particular types of tasks and function efficiently on others.

Everyone procrastinates occasionally, putting off something that ought to be done now. But to earn the title of procrastinator, people have to *habitually* postpone doing tasks they feel ought to be done immediately.

Where do you fit into the procrastination picture? Remember, we all procrastinate occasionally, but for the chronic procrastinator, procrastination is a way of life.

Take a few minutes and answer the following Procrastination Survey. (Don't put it off!) Answer as honestly as you can. At the end of the survey, you will learn where you fit on the procrastination spectrum.

PROCRASTINATION SURVEY

	Yes	No
1. Do you feel resentful when someone reminds you of tasks you have left undone?		
2. Do you feel you have too much to do each day?		
3. Do you find yourself frequently making excuses for work unfinished?		
4. Do you spend time on nonessentials while letting important work go?		
5. Do you sometimes delay a task so long that you're embarrassed to do it?		
6. Do you use high energy times for low priority tasks?		
7. Do you often have a hard time determining what to do first?		

15

8. Do you often make promises—to your-self, to others, to God—and then fail to keep them? ____ ____
9. Do you sometimes agree to do a task and then regret it? ____ ____
10. Do you often fail to list tasks you agree to do? ____ ____
11. Do you think you work better under pressure? ____ ____
12. Do you put off doing your income tax form until April? ____ ____
13. Do you almost always feel in a hurry? ____ ____
14. Do you continue to work on tasks even when they are as good as they need to be? ____ ____
15. Do you sometimes think that by wait-ing long enough the tasks will not have to be done? ____ ____
16. Do you have difficulty saying no to people? ____ ____
17. Do you think more about the one complaint than the many compli-ments? ____ ____
18. Do you feel frustrated much of the time? ____ ____
19. Do you feel guilty while playing? ____ ____
20. Do you forget to write down what you agree to do? ____ ____

Procrastination Factor

Give yourself five points for each Yes answer and total your score.

0 – 20.   Efficiency expert
25 – 40.   Doing well

YOU CAN CHANGE

How did you do? Did you qualify as a full-blown chronic procrastinator? Don't despair. There is hope! You can acquire new attitudes and skills that will help you to stop procrastinating and start living.

I know that procrastination patterns can be changed. I've learned the lessons the hard way, by dealing with my own procrastination. My research has taught me much about the causes and cures for procrastination. I have taught these methods to hundreds of people in procrastination seminars that have dramatically changed people's lives.

George, a plumber who works for a government agency during the day and moonlights his trade every evening and weekends, not only started requiring appointments for services, but started courting his wife and playing with his children. He discovered two things: 1) he didn't have time for everything, and 2) his family was the most important value in his life.

Alice, a homemaker, had the unreasonable expectation of being able to have a dustless house. She was almost killing herself trying to keep the house clean. After adjusting her attitudes and devising a plan, she greeted her husband every evening with a smile on her face, ready to enjoy his company. "At six o'clock the tired housewife image gave way to the comfortable wife and lively lover," she said.

A year after he attended a seminar, Jim met me in a restaurant and told me that his fantasy of 20 years had

17

come true—he had started his own business and was operating it successfully.

Three months after completing a seminar, Al proudly told the follow-up group that he had converted his boss to a nonprocrastination style of life and that the engineering firm had become a pleasant place to work.

Instead of bolting from his desk to every parishioner who said "I need to see you," Reverend Allen started asking "Is it an emergency?" If not (and most were not), he suggested a more convenient time for a conference with the parishioner.

Bob, an architect, decided that life was too short to spend eight hours a day listening to a tyrannical boss humiliate people. He quit.

One of the most exciting programs was instituted with Barry Benton, a prosecuting attorney for the Fayette County Court System in Lexington, Kentucky. Benton arranged with the courts to offer people arrested for writing "cold" checks an alternative to the normal procedure. For the crime of failing math or putting off balancing a checkbook in Fayette County the normal procedure was: first offense—a fine plus court cost plus a criminal record; second offense—the above plus a 30-day jail sentence. During this program violators were given the option of accepting the above or attending a four-day seminar on procrastination. Though the participants began the first meeting hostile, they usually concluded the seminar thanking the courts for the opportunity of attending the seminar, with many promising to keep in touch with other members of the group.

In a final evaluation of a seminar, a pastor wrote:

> I no longer look at procrastination as simply
> a tendency to put off tasks, a kind of laugh-
> able habit, a matter of little concern except

that I might get more work done if I didn't have that funny quirk. I can now see procrastination for what it is, a life-style guaranteed to breed frustration—indeed, a personal and spiritual disease that threatens effective living. I came in seeking tools; I came away embracing a theory. I also came away with a workshop full of tools. I am still a long way from being a recovered procrastinator, but I am learning to use the tools. I am recovering. I can look at myself with a degree of hope. I feel better about myself, and I feel more relaxed. I no longer feel I must pressure myself to achieve; I know I can achieve without the pressure. I know now it is possible to be in control of my life.

I have found that the cures for procrastination work better and faster for those who take the time to understand procrastination and its causes before they try to change their ways of working and relating to people. Therefore in the next chapter we will take a closer look at the procrastinator. What kind of a person is this?

2

Profile of the Procrastinator

Earl, account executive for a dairy, was a charming, pleasant person who cultivated friendships with customers. His boyish, nonthreatening, accepting attitude caused others to trust him. His skill of discovering a person's hobby and discussing it without knowing anything about it was uncanny. Earl appeared to be as harmless as homogenized milk.

Though Earl gained many new customers for the company, he had one problem. After promising to do something for a customer, he would write himself a note on a scrap of paper, a paper napkin, or the inside of a matchbook cover. Earl really intended to do what he promised the customer, but he often "forgot" to follow through. Weeks later he would dig up from a coat pocket a note that reminded him that he had missed the opportunity to keep his promise. He knew that the customer would now be angry and begin to listen to the mating call of the competition.

Earl is a good example of a procrastinator. With other procrastinators he shares certain characteristics. I have identified 17. Not all these will apply to all people who procrastinate, but a general picture emerges.

1. *Procrastinators do not have a manageable way of organizing their time and tasks.* Even procrastinators who make To Do Lists, with a firm resolve to follow the lists,

often become victims of administration by impulse, *responding* to what happens to them rather than *causing* things to happen.

2. *Procrastinators have good intentions.* They really believe they are going to do what they agree to do. Ten minutes after saying yes, they often regret the decision.

3. *Procrastinators usually have a bundle of excuses.* Rare is the person who says, "I didn't do what I promised to do for you. No excuses. No reasons. I just didn't do it." If one of our ways of working with others causes conflict, we discover ways to survive and, if possible, save face. So excuses emerge: "I didn't have time to do it. You should see my schedule; it would kill a workaholic."

There is an exception to the "excuse me" rule. It is used by people who disarm their critics by attacking themselves before their critics can. I have a friend who uses the confessional method effectively. He is a master of self-effacing confession without losing face, which is not an easy skill to develop.

4. *Procrastinators are charming people.* This is one way procrastinators cope with the consequences of their procrastination. They are pleasant, often appeasing, and appear to enjoy the companionship of others. A nice person is not a threat to others. People do not have to worry about them causing conflict in public by rudely contradicting what is said or by stomping angrily out of a meeting. (The procrastinator may not be that charming at home.)

5. *Procrastinators have difficulty saying no.* Smiling, they often agree to do anything for anyone, even at great personal sacrifice; but they don't or can't fulfill the promises.

6. *Procrastinators trade a feeling of victory for one of relief.* Because they put off tasks until the last minute,

21

procrastinators go through life trying to relieve tension and to seek tranquility by eliminating that which irritates. Much of life is lived *reacting* to the negative rather than *acting* to create a positive difference in oneself and between oneself and others. Procrastinators rarely can celebrate with a feeling of accomplishment, and the feeling of relief is short-lived because there are always other tasks ready to kill the feeling and assume top billing in the "ought to" department.

7. *Procrastinators focus on the negative*—on what is not done rather than on what they are doing. They may plan to complete eight important tasks for the day, complete six of them, and then feel defeated because of the two undone tasks instead of being happy with the six finished projects. They remember the one complaint and forget the ten compliments.

8. *Procrastinators think they can do better than they show.* They create a fantasized self-image—"I am more talented, more competent, and more intellectual than I show." This may be true, but by waiting until the last minute to complete a task and thereby having to rush, procrastinators never have to admit their limitations and will never know for sure what they can accomplish.

9. *Procrastinators seldom use evaluation to improve performance.* Whenever possible, they avoid criticism of any kind. Even if given, criticism can be rationalized; "I could have performed *if* I had had more time. I'm too busy to look back; I have to catch up with yesterday's undone deed." Yet, there is a haunting suspicion that if one does his or her best, it will not measure up to standards.

10. *Procrastinators expend much of their energy and time worrying about what they should be doing.* Worrying uses much of the energy needed to accomplish important tasks and then to celebrate. Preoccupation with

the past (what I should have done) and the future (what I must do) leaves one numbly suspended between the two.

11. *Procrastinators are seldom emotionally and intellectually totally present at any moment.* When playing, they think about work ("I have a million things to do, and here I am playing bridge"). Often while working, procrastinators think about playing ("I can just see the bass breaking the water. A soft cast under a low-hanging cypress tree limb and *pow*—a six-pound trophy"). Even when working on easy tasks to avoid doing a difficult task, they cannot escape for long the nagging thought that they ought to be working on the difficult task.

12. *Procrastinators feel overwhelmed.* Their minds are muddled with everything that ought to be done at once. Because all tasks feel like one enormous impossible burden, procrastinators feel overwhelmed. A cartoon depicted a woman slouched in a lounge chair, bathrobe loosely draped over her body, hair in curlers, looking exhausted when her husband returned from work. Looking up at her husband, she said, "I had so much to do that I didn't know where to start. . . . So I didn't." That is the recurring feeling and action of a procrastinator.

13. *Procrastinators look for others to rescue them.* As Jim expressed it, "In the back of my mind I keep hoping that if I wait a little longer, I won't have to do the job— that somehow it will disappear. Maybe someone will decide that it doesn't need doing, or someone else will do it, or the need for the job will cease to exist." Procrastinators are rescued by spouses, bosses, co-workers, and friends often enough to perpetuate the wishful thinking.

14. *Procrastinators claim to work better under pressure.* "It seems that I just can't get the mental and emotional machinery revved up enough to get the job done until it is deadline time," explained John. "I even schedule way

ahead of the deadline and sit down to do the task, but nothing happens. Yet, when the pressure is on and I *have* to get it done, I put out the work. The quality of work may not be the best, but the quantity is amazing. I just work better under pressure." Many procrastinators produce best under pressure and often only under pressure. This does not totally compensate them, however, for they are rarely satisfied with the pressurized product.

15. *Procrastinators resent being reminded.* Describing his reaction to his mother when he was 12 years old, Ralph said, "Every time she reminded me to do something, especially take out the garbage, I became firmer in my resolve not to do it." The note from the boss reminding Sid of an overdue report caused a similar reaction. "If he would quit sending those notes I would get the report finished. But every time I receive one of those reminders, I postpone the job as long as possible." When we are reminded of what we think and feel we should have already done, it triggers something in us, and that something is usually resentment.

16. *Procrastinators have a low self-image.* This way of being, playing, and working with people affects the way we feel about ourselves and others, and those feelings are difficult to live with. The feelings often expressed by procrastinators are guilt, depression, frustration, resentment, hostility, self-pity, self-disgust, disappointment, and fear (of embarrassment, rejection, and failure). Procrastinating behavior and the resulting feelings create a low self-image. Much of the time procrastinators do not like themselves.

17. *Procrastinators often feel powerless.* They do not want to irritate others or handicap themselves with procrastination, yet they often feel powerless to change the way they are and the environment in which they work and live.

To help you apply the ideas in this chapter, use the above checklist of the 17 characteristics of the procrastinator. As you read over them, note the ones you think apply to you. It may be helpful to do this with another person. Let each one identify his or her own problems, "confess" to one another, and then contract to help one another overcome the problem of procrastination.

Part Two

The Causes of Procrastination

3

The Quest
for Perfection

Don's poised, relaxed body transformed into a rigid, tense, hostile arsenal when he began talking about his mother. "My mother was impossible. She still is. It seemed that everything I did had to be done perfect, no matter how insignificant the task. A good example is the wastebaskets. It was my chore to empty the eight wastebaskets in the house. One time she had to hunt for a piece of paper, and sure enough, she found a tag off a dress shirt clinging to the bottom of a wicker basket. With basket in hand she marched up to me, shoved the basket under my face, pointed to the tag, and said, 'Can't you do anything right?' Not once did she load her arms with the seven empty baskets and say, 'Good job, son.' She never mentioned the things I did right, only the failures, and she could find a way to make anything a failure. So I quit trying to please her and put off doing what she wanted me to until she had a temper tantrum."

While sitting in a restaurant with several friends, I mentioned what I was beginning to suspect about procrastinator's parents. To the embarrassment of the rest of us, George responded, "You're right! My father was never satisfied with anything I did. We were painting the inside of the house; I was painting the bedroom a light green over white. After it dried, he inspected the room. I missed

29

a small spot in a corner near the ceiling, about four inches square. He made me paint the whole wall over—not the spot, the whole wall! And when I finished repainting it he said, 'That's the way you should have done it in the first place.' I never did anything that satisfied him."

John, 36, calmly explained that his father was a perfectionist. John and his brother reacted differently to their father. Even as a small child, his brother openly fought with his father, stubbornly refusing to do what his father ordered. John said, "I always wanted to please my father, so I tried to do what he asked. Yet, I never seemed to please him. If he had to look under the chrome, he would find a speck of dirt on the car after I washed it. Even today I dread to visit my parents because I know he will find something to criticize. My parents are coming to visit next week, and already I'm dreading it. Before the week's over he'll have something to say about the paint on the house, or the car, or the children. Within 30 minutes after arriving, he'll ask me when I had the oil changed in the car. When I am around him, I change completely; I regress to the little boy nervously trying to please his daddy. It's degrading."

PERFECTIONISTS AND
PROCRASTINATION

John and his physician brother were programmed by the same parents, but they reacted in opposite ways to the same stimulus: John procrastinated; his brother tried to be perfect. Procrastinators and perfectionists are conditioned by the same early responses to them by parents or parental substitutes, and each day ends with both of them feeling the same way—incomplete, dissatisfied with their efforts, and, at least partially, like failures. Both feel compelled to perform perfectly, for procrastinators are perfectionists in disguise.

Perfectionists and procrastinators were reared by parents or parental substitutes who focused on the negative, what was inadequately done, or who set too high a standard with their accomplishments. In the latter case, the children felt inadequate, not because of what parents said, but by the way their parents performed tasks and accomplished "great" acts.

Out of the hundreds of procrastinators I interviewed, only two had parents who were "too perfect" to emulate. The others came from homes where parents pointed to the failure of the child. If the child made six A's and one B on the report card, mother or father pointed to the B and said, "You can do better than that." If the child mowed two acres of lawn and missed six inches in the back corner, father said, "See. You can do better than that." If the child successfully washed the dishes, mother noticed that she couldn't see her reflection in the plates or called attention to the crumbs on the table.

"Never be satisfied with what you do, because you can do better next time, if you really want to," these parents say. All through life procrastinators hear the little saboteur of satisfaction whispering, "You can do better . . . you can do better . . . you can do better." The victim may or may not be conscious of it, but the message is there.

A difference between procrastinators and perfectionists is in the response they make to the message. Perfectionists say, "I'll show you. I'll do it perfectly." Procrastinators say, "Why try? No matter what I do it won't be good enough."

Procrastinators and perfectionists live with the same dilemma. Either the task is produced perfectly, or it is a failure. Partial success and partial failure are not accep-

31

table. Whether the procrastinator or the perfectionist is painting a house or a portrait, the job must be perfect.

DWELLING ON THE NEGATIVE

From childhood procrastinators have been trained to seek out and to dwell on the blemish, the flaw, the incomplete deed, the complaint. Where our parents left off, we pick up. Though they may not be with us, our parents' way of viewing life is our constant companion—that is, unless we decide to change.

An efficient executive could have been satisfied with the citations on his wall, the power of his position, and the outstanding accomplishments to his credit, but he was dissatisfied with himself. Though he got things done and did them well, he thought of himself as a procrastinator and resented the pressure he put on himself.

When I examined his current year's schedule and his projected schedule for the following year, I discovered that he was a very organized person. On a typical day he listed 20 important tasks to complete. By the end of the day he usually had completed 17 or 18 of them—a good day's work filled with significant accomplishments. Yet, he felt defeated daily. For he didn't think about what he had accomplished; he moped about what he failed to do.

Procrastinators are programmed to stare at the incompleted tasks and only glance at the completed ones. So no matter how much or how good the procrastinator does, it is not good enough. Within the procrastinator is a *feeling* of incompleteness hunting for an excuse to justify its existence. At best, a no-win situation haunts procrastinators with the saboteur saying, "You can do better."

PERFECTIONISM AND THE CHURCH

Many parents were trained in this perfectionistic view of life by the church. With an occasional nod to what is

32

right with people, the church has often focused on what is wrong with them. In an overzealous desire to help people overcome that which hurts them, the church has often majored in the blemish business, with the laborious litany "You can do better."

The consequences of this view of life are usually disastrous in two ways.

First, so long as we teach people to stare at their blemishes, there is going to be an army of guilt-ridden, frustrated, perpetually dissatisfied people searching for blemishes in others instead of appreciating the good, beautiful, and right about them. They will forget the hundred little acts of kindness and dwell on the one forgotten birthday. They will mourn those who are absent from the meeting instead of celebrating those who made it. They will be condemned to looking at blemishes and miss most of the beauty.

Second, people who devote all their efforts to coping with unruly agendas hardly have time to notice people for the people's sake. Procrastinators are often too busy trying to cope with all those "oughts" to think about what is best for other people. There is seldom time to take a break from oneself—no time to relax, reflect, and be renewed by a healthy interest in others. Even playing with the children or doing charitable work gets tainted with an "ought to" instead of a fun "want to."

Some of the perfectionism preaching from parents and pulpit is the result of a misunderstanding of the word *perfect* as used in the Bible. In Matthew 5:46-48 Jesus speaks of loving enemies and then concludes, "You, therefore, must be perfect as your heavenly Father is perfect." There are three meanings of the word translated *perfect*.

First, *perfect* has to do with attitudes and actions towards people. The parallel passage in Luke 6:36 reads, "Be merciful even as your Father is merciful." To be perfect is to consider the thoughts, feelings, and needs of others in our dealings with them. It does not mean that everything must meet some flawless criteria; it does mean that we are to care about people as God does.

Second, *perfect* is not a static condition. It implies a process of growth, of change. Perfect suggests a dynamic growing towards increasing sensitivity to others. Though we are not perfect all the time, we can demonstrate perfection (mercy) much of the time. When we show mercy, we are perfect for that act and in that moment.

Third, *perfect* suggests an attitude that relieves us from thinking about ourselves all the time. So long as we try to be perfect to please others or God, we keep ourselves the center of the universe. To be perfect in the biblical sense means that God frees us to think and care about others.

4

But I'm Afraid

A second major cause for procrastination is fear. The most obvious is fear of failure. Often we put off a certain task because consciously or unconsciously we are afraid to fail, afraid we won't do it well enough. But there are two other major fears as well: the fear of success (strange as it may seem) and the fear of rejection.

FEAR OF FAILURE

People tend to procrastinate when they are unsure of their skill to perform the task satisfactorily. With the possibility of failure increased by the lack of confidence and skill, procrastinators' ability to predict the outcome is lessened and their anxiety increased. Waiting until there is not enough time to complete the task before the deadline, procrastinators often say, "If I can't do it right, I won't do it at all."

As an executive in a major denomination, Bill counsels pastors, consults with congregational leaders, coordinates continuing programs, administers the overall program for hundreds of church organizations, and represents his denomination on the international religious scene. After 28 years in the administrative position, Bill is secure in his job. And rightly so, because he gets the job done with a slight handicap. Bill does not like to write letters. Because he anticipates additional questions and sees the many sides of an issue, Bill cannot write a concise, clear letter; life is not that simple to Bill.

In my research more people mentioned procrastinating on letter writing than on any other act. There are at least two explanations for this.

First, the lack of skill causes people to evade the responsibility. Procrastinators use such phrases as "I can't express myself clearly in writing," "I'm not sure how to say what I want to say," and "I can never seem to get the first sentence right." Obviously, many people postpone writing the important letter because they do not think they have the skill to write well enough to express what they think.

Second, some are reluctant to commit themselves by putting their thoughts on paper. A professor I greatly admired never wrote a word, which is a great loss to the world. He explained, "I don't want to be accused of believing something I don't believe. By the time the article or book appears in print I may have discovered new evidence which could cause me to change my mind." As one person said, "When you put your thoughts on paper, it seems so final."

In addition to letter-writing, here are some other situations in which people are prone to procrastinate.

Some people procrastinate when the act involves asking for a favor. Some people feel demeaned when asking for a favor, for the asking of a favor suggests that the other person is in control of the relationship. With head humbly bowed—symbolically, if not actually—one awaits the denial or granting of the gift.

Some people procrastinate visiting an ill person. Many people are uncomfortable when visiting someone physically ill. This discomfort is caused by two things: the visitor does not know what to say or do, and the visitor does not want to think about becoming ill. When some people think about visiting a friend with an emotionally disabling condition, they approach a feeling of panic.

Some people procrastinate visiting bereaved people, so they depend on Hallmark to say it for them. By sending a card they don't have to see, hear, and feel the grief of others or view the body of the deceased and be reminded of their own death.

Lack of skill—real or imaginary—causes people to postpone particular tasks. The reason offered is that they are waiting until they have sufficient time and resources to do the job right, because "If I can't do it right, I won't do it at all." The lack of skill is a valid reason for shelving a task, but some tasks demand attention and refuse to be dismissed until action is taken to resolve the problem.

Because some people are afraid of failure, *they put off starting a job until they have more information.* This search for more information may go on endlessly.

"When it appears that I am procrastinating, I am not really," explained Mac. "I examine the details of a project in my mind while waiting until I have all the information I need to complete the project. Though I know what I'm doing, others affected by my action or inaction do not, and they often get nervous. After 18 years of seeing me come through at the last minute, Martha, my wife, still worries about me making it in the stretch.

"Recently, we decided to build a playroom on the house. No less than 20 times she asked, 'When are you going to see the bank about the loan for the playroom?' When I told her I was working on the plans to determine how much money we needed, she didn't believe me because she couldn't see my mind working. She nagged me. I got irritated, and we had a fight over something that was supposed to make us happy. I'm the kind of person who doesn't want to take the first step until I have all the information I need to do the job."

One management expert complains that research is the biggest bottleneck in industry. Though research is essential, especially to satisfy government regulations and to insure product control and sales potential, research people have a tendency to fondle a fact to death. Researchers want all the answers to every possible question before stating a conclusion or acting on an idea, which is understandable. Researching is their business, not selling. The hunt is the fun, not the end product.

Waiting until one has *all* the information needed to make a decision or to start action on a project is a luxury few people can enjoy. Few situations offer absolute information to solve problems perfectly. The unpredictability of people and processes makes it impossible to predict the future perfectly. Because of the fear of failure, procrastinators often defer action until all information is in. Sometimes then it is too late to use the pearls of wisdom, or procrastinators throw them together hurriedly into a jumbled pile because they don't have time to string them.

FEAR OF SUCCESS

Some people procrastinate because they fear success. This fear is fostered by the expectation that the more one achieves the more one is expected to achieve.

Many organizations are crowded at the middle-management level with people who are more skilled and creative than they show. Because they accomplish more than people with less talent, even though they procrastinate habitually, they remain in the middle-management position. Consciously or unconsciously, these people choose to remain in that position, because they do not want the additional pressure that comes with greater efficiency and more responsibility. Few people tell their boss, "I am giving the company only 70 percent of my ability. I can do much better. I could increase sales 25 percent in 12 months, but if I do, you will probably promote me to district sales manager. Because I have all the pressure I can stand right now, I don't want that job."

The one unforgivable sin in an achievement-oriented society is to do less than one can, to not produce to the maximum of one's capacity. This ideal creates tension in people who do not like the pressure of having to compete against themselves and beat last year's record.

Procrastinators are caught in a dilemma. With more ability than they demonstrate, they often feel guilty for not living up to their potential. Others often recognize their innate ability and wisdom and try to motivate procrastinators with such words as, "You have the potential to be great in court. You could be a famous lawyer if you applied yourself." "With a little extra effort you could be the best quarterback in the league." "With more determination you can make the dean's list."

Thelma said, "If one more person tells me that I have great potential, I will stuff my briefcase in his mouth. People think they are encouraging you when they talk about your potential. All they do is put more pressure on you. What do they know? I just may be doing my best. Can't people be satisfied with what I give them?"

Procrastinators are caught between the fear of additional responsibility—thus a greater chance of failing—and the pressure to do their best. When they do not try their hardest, they often feel guilty. The solution is to do one's best at the last minute. This reaction is not usually a conscious decision; it is a psychic response to a tough problem, and the response is not without its rewards. Top administrators do not usually appoint procrastinators as chairpersons of committees or assign them to direct major projects. Efficient people are often saddled with extra work, and not always with extra pay.

When I mentioned this idea to Suzanne, she exploded with a tirade about two "lazy girls" who worked in the same secretarial pool with her. Suzanne and another secretary are overworked, while the two lazy secretaries fiddle most of their time away. Because they procrastinate, the two "lazy girls" are rewarded; they are given less work to do and do not have to type the more stress-producing documents which have a close deadline.

Some people procrastinate because they do not want the extra responsibility, additional work, and increased pressure that snowballs with success. Procrastination is a reasonable solution to a problem for a person who does not want to live like a high achiever; the problem is solved without losing face. Some procrastinators are not physically, emotionally, and intellectually equipped to be high achievers. Yet, they have been cursed with an image of themselves that demands perfection. While the type of goal varies greatly, from manicured lawns and bicycle repairs to trying to beat the international monetary game, the results are the same: persons dissatisfied with themselves because they failed to do what they thought they could.

People who procrastinate to ward off too much success trade one kind of pressure for another cause of tension. They trade external pressure caused by success for the tension created by procrastinating.

FEAR OF REJECTION

Larry is a minister of a congregation in the South. Members of this congregation proudly point to their "preacher," subtly hinting to their friends, who are members of another denomination, that Larry is superior to their minister.

Larry's serene smile, subtle sense of humor, spontaneous laughter, and pleasant manner disarms people. With square shoulders and erect posture, Larry's athletic body, draped with impeccably matched clothing, gives the appearance of efficiency. He *looks* efficient. Larry's poise and confidence add to the picture of properness. He *sounds* efficient. His sermons are logical, clear, and concise. Each word is in place, each thought naturally leads to the next thought.

But Larry has a problem that causes him and others much confusion and agony: he cannot say no to any request. In addition, Larry seeks community causes and clubs to join, and he volunteers for tasks. Oh yes, Larry will *agree* to do anything for anybody at any time; but he does not do it, or he does it late. His saving grace is that when he apologizes for not doing what he promised to do, the person who asked him to do the deed feels guilty for having asked.

Procrastinators often agree to do more than they can possibly do because they are reluctant to say no to requests. They say *yes* when they feel *no* because of their need for approval, the desire to be liked, complimented, and reassured by others. People with a strong need for approval are often controlled by the opinions of others.

Approval is often sought in all areas of life, from personal appearance to proper performance. To have to be all things to all people is another impossible form of perfection, for no matter how one acts, or which side of an issue one takes, some people will approve and others will disapprove. This is a dilemma for procrastinators who have a strong need for approval.

Approval-motivated people avoid interpersonal conflict if at all possible, because conflict may cause personal rejection. A recent survey revealed that most people's greatest fear is personal rejection, rated ahead of physical pain and even death. This fear of rejection causes procrastinators to say yes when they mean no.

The need for approval may cause procrastination in another way. Some people procrastinate because of peer pressure. To be outstanding—to set the curve in a college course, to be identified as the brightest or the prettiest or the greatest in any way—is to invite jealousy and criticism from one's peers. The safest place is in the middle, not too smart or too dumb, never too conspicuous. For many people the important thing is to be well liked, and procrastination is a convenient, safe way for people to stay in the middle and be approved.

One person explained how this happens in the office where she works:

> If a person starts putting out too much work,
> displays too much skill and acts enthusiastic,
> the other women let her know real fast that
> she had better slow down. If she doesn't, no
> one speaks to her.

The results are that a conscientious secretary is pressured into conforming to the lowest denominator, with everyone giving only half of what she has. The same dynamic can be found everywhere, from assembly line workers to middle-management executives.

So long as you fear rejection by others, you are not free to choose according to your own values and goals. While you may never overcome this fear entirely, you can learn that you don't have to please everyone all the time. That is only another form of perfectionism.

5

Living with the Brakes On

When a car is driven with the brakes on, it wastes fuel, burns up brake drums, and puts additional strain on the engine. The automobile does not perform efficiently, and it wears out sooner than it was intended to.

So it is with people who habitually procrastinate. The tension between what *ought* to be done, and when one *wants* to do what, produces a life-style of living with the brakes on. With two thoughts driving the human engine ("I have to be perfect" vs. "I can't be perfect, so I will wait until later to try"), procrastinators live with "you *ought* to do it now" fighting "I don't *want* to do it now." The inner tension uses much of the energy and creativity needed to do the job adequately.

This tension is inevitable for procrastinators in an achievement-oriented society where personal worth is equated with how much and how well one achieves. Most people are conditioned early in life to believe in "salvation by works." The greater the achievement, the greater the salvation. Achieving to assure self-worth can be in any area of life, from cooking a delicious cheese soufflé to managing a large conglomerate. Almost every task is a measure of personal worth for the procrastinator—all life is being judged. The formula is simple: if you achieve sufficiently, people will reward you with pay, praise, and prestige; and if other people say so, then you must be a worthy person.

Procrastinators can feel good about themselves only when they achieve adequately. But "you can do better" always judges harshly, and procrastinators often feel like failures in many areas of life.

ACHIEVEMENT-MOTIVATED PEOPLE

We can understand procrastinators better if we compare them with achievement-motivated people.

1. *Achievement-motivated people need goals to prove their worth.* They identify themselves primarily by their accomplishments: chairperson of the United Fund, top salesperson in the firm, scholar of 1982, winner of the Tournament of Champions, secretary of the church women's group, best bridge player in the neighborhood. In an achievement-oriented society most people are conditioned to believe their personal worth is determined by how much and how well they achieve certain goals. Because of this, procrastinators have a love-hate relationship with goals. They need goals, yet resent them, because the criteria they use make adequate achieving nearly impossible.

2. *Achievement-motivated people need goals that are difficult enough to challenge them.* When goals are too easy, achievers lose interest. Procrastinators accept and claim challenging goals and then try to accomplish them with a minimum of time and energy, which usually assures a less-than-perfect performance.

3. *Achievement-motivated people need new goals that are more challenging than previous goals.* Accomplishing the same thing over and over does not interest high achievers.

Because one level of success demands a greater degree of accomplishment, procrastinators are ambivalent about

44

succeeding, which causes them to try to move full speed ahead with the brakes on.

FIDDLING AROUND

If one procrastinates, how are achievement needs met? Fortunately procrastinators always have a backlog of tasks. Avoiding difficult tasks until they have to be done, procrastinators work on easier tasks to salve their consciences temporarily and to give themselves some satisfaction from achieving.

Bill was asked to have a quarterly report ready by October 26. On October 25 Bill took the material home to write the report. After dinner, he fussed with figures and phrases for two hours. According to Bill, "At nine o'clock something inside seemed to snap, and I kicked out of balance, like a computer gone wild. Tossing those papers aside I started working crossword puzzles. Crossword puzzles are my hobby. I'm ashamed to admit it, but I worked crossword puzzles for hours." Sharply at three A.M. Bill tossed the crossword puzzle book on the sofa and picked up the report. With a sigh of relief he placed the period on the last sentence at seven A.M.

Does this sound ridiculous? Bill thinks so. He was embarrassed to admit such behavior. But it is not unlike people who straighten desk debris and write thank-you notes for last year's Christmas gifts while avoiding a more important but difficult task. Doing easy tasks sometimes produces a feeling of accomplishment, clears the cobwebs from the mind, temporarily, and sometimes builds confidence for the challenging job ahead. But too often "fiddling around" produces only frustration, a poor substitute for the feeling of accomplishment gained by the achievement-minded person.

6

Too Much
or Too Little

Some people have more to do than they can get done in the specified time. There is not enough time to complete correspondence, return telephone calls, write reports, meet clients, attend meetings, etc. There are not enough hours in a day to cook three meals, vacuum the house, wash and dry clothes, rock a baby, attend church activities, collect for the Cancer Fund, answer letters, write checks, drive a daughter to Little League baseball practice and a son to drama class, etc. Combine the professional and family responsibilities, and two people are going to be overscheduled and feel overwhelmed.

When people have too much to do, there is usually a constant inner battle accompanied by tensions over priorities and time management. Pastors live daily with the dilemma, "Do I attend the United Fund Campaign luncheon, or visit Alec in the hospital, or work on the sermon, or write the stewardship letter, or design the Day Care Center brochure, or call on the new couple who attended church Sunday? All *have* to be done. What *won't* I do?" Five minutes after the priorities have been set, Mr. Jones telephones to say that he and Martha have decided to get a divorce and must see the pastor immediately. As the pastor rises to leave, another telephone call reports a death. The beautiful plans of the organized pastor sail out the window, but the tasks will wait.

Many people have too much to do and procrastinate on tasks because they cannot complete them on time. If these people are not organized and do not set priorities, they respond by impulse. Whatever gets their attention gets their time and energy. Being bounced between duties like a loose balloon bounced from person to person at a football game, these people aimlessly react to others. At the end of the day, half-written letters, scribbled notes, and a legion of "To Do's" whisper, "You ought to be ashamed of yourself."

Sometimes too much to do is built into the job portfolio. Often in an effort to spring into success, one grabs more responsibility than one person can manage successfully.

TOO LITTLE TO DO

Ralph quit his job, reduced the number of courses he was taking in graduate school, and assured himself that in summer school he was going to improve his grades. Thinking that with less responsibility he would have all class work completed ahead of time, he would redeem himself with patient professors, and, more importantly, with himself. Taking a light course load would also free him to play with his wife and children more. Happy with his decision, he knew that he would not only finish term papers ahead of schedule, but he would produce a perfect, polished product every time.

Much to his dismay, the summer semester rolled by him without his noticing. Just as it was about out of sight, he frantically cranked out papers and read books until the deadline. Bleary-eyed from lack of sleep, he asked one professor for a four-day extension.

Not having enough to do tempts one to procrastinate more than having too much to do. Procrastinators seem to manage a crowded schedule better than a lonely one, because procrastinators usually finish what they *have* to do when they *have* to.

Ralph followed the easy summer with a schedule that only a masochist would plan. It amounted to about an 80-hour work and school week, family and recreation not included. When I suggested that he would manage it well, he thought I was out of my mind. "If I can't handle a 30-hour week, how can I manage an 80-hour one?"

"You will," I replied.

Four months later he was beaming with pride. He had managed, and he did so because deadlines were almost daily, and he did not have time to indulge in his perfectionism. He did the best he could with the time available.

Procrastinators use the time they have to finish a task. If the task is due in two weeks, they foster the illusion that they have plenty of time and then wait until they dread doing the deed and rush to complete it. Procrastinators produce the same quality of work whether they have two days or two weeks to complete the task, because they wait until the pressure pushes them into action.

Too little to do has another side-effect, which has to do with the energy to do what needs doing. Interest in a task generates the energy to complete it. Interest is the motor that stimulates ideas and energy.

The reverse is also true. Boring, unpleasant, routine tasks sap energy. When procrastinators have too much time to do the job, they usually fiddle the time away dreading the boring task. Dreading to do something usually takes more energy than doing it.

KEEPING BUSY

In addition to the causes of procrastination already mentioned, there is another cause operating here. Sarah explained:

> I intentionally postpone finishing tasks, because I don't want to finish. This has nothing to do with liking or disliking what I am doing. I think the *doing* of something is better than not doing at all. For instance, eight guests were coming for dinner last week. I was up early vacuuming, dusting, preparing food, and planning other necessary activities. By three o'clock I was almost finished. The roast was in the oven, and everything was in order, except one cleaning job. The desk in the dining room was covered with papers which needed organizing and filing. I purposely avoided clearing the desk until just before the guests were to arrive.

Sarah explained that she had a love-hate relationship with work. She wanted to relax more, but couldn't. "I need unfinished business to keep me busy," she reported.

Sarah needs a load of undone, unpleasant duties to prevent her from enjoying life. Sarah is a charming person, with unusual insights into motivation, who accomplishes much. She also lingers on painful projects to perpetuate her need to suffer. The profile fits the programming of many procrastinators; they are conditioned to plan their pain and failure.

Procrastinators have difficulty using free time or play time to energize themselves. Thus, an overcrowded schedule is easier to manage than a lonely one.

7

Power Through Procrastination

Barry is the administrator of a government agency with a budget in excess of 100 million dollars. Once he interviewed a young lawyer who was interested in "serving the people." Neat in appearance and obviously intelligent, the lawyer responded to questions quickly and concisely without being confrontive. He was self-confident, had a keen sense of humor, liked people, and seemed to thrive on problems. After the interview, it seemed to Barry that this man was ideal for the job. He would relieve the pressure Barry felt from legal problems; he was brimming over with program ideas; he was wise in the political games government agencies have to play.

Barry sent for the lawyer's references. They read as if the man's mother had written them. Anxious to share the good news with the personnel director, Barry telephoned him. The director was out, so Barry sent the references with his notes suggesting that the lawyer be hired. Across the first page he wrote RUSH.

A week later, Barry sent another memo asking if the lawyer had been hired. "Still processing the papers," was the reply.

"Please rush it. We don't want to lose this man," Barry wrote across the face of the memo and returned it to the personnel director.

50

Another week passed without any action. Barry tried to see the director three times, but each time he was in conference. Finally, Barry left a note telling the director to contact him before he left that day. When the director telephoned, he told Barry that the lawyer did not qualify for the job because he didn't have the proper college degree. Barry *told* him to find a way around the regulation and "have him hired when I return from Washington next Wednesday."

Upon returning from Washington Barry learned that the lawyer had not been hired, and that the personnel director had left the day before on a three-week vacation. Barry asked the assistant director to come to his office; he explained the situation to her. Fifteen minutes later he had the information he needed to hire the lawyer.

Barry said, "Then I realized that the personnel director had no intention of hiring that man." After we analyzed the situation, Barry was angry because he realized that the personnel director had said "nobody tells me what to do" without opening his mouth. There wasn't anything Barry could do about it; the personnel director was a political appointee.

Procrastination can be an expression of personal power as well as a way of rebelling against authority. All people need personal power to survive, and if they don't get power one way, they find other ways to influence people. Personal power is:

- a husband pouting until his wife, who thinks a night in the Ramada Inn is roughing it, agrees to camp out for their vacation.
- a wife nagging until her husband, through gritted teeth says, "OK, OK, I give up. Get dressed; we'll go out for a happy anniversary dinner."

51

- a personnel director not processing the papers to hire a person even though his boss has told him to do it.

Procrastination can be a way of influencing those in authority. Several people interviewed smiled when this possibility was mentioned. Reviewing the effects their procrastination had on their "superiors" (bosses, spouses, teachers, parents), these people felt a little embarrassed yet had trouble suppressing a smirk. While feeling relatively powerless to effect certain changes, they were nevertheless influencing others. In a self-defeating way procrastination satisfies some people's need for power, which is supposed to enhance self-esteem. This way of influencing others does not enhance self-esteem, it merely enables one to flex a flabby muscle.

Procrastination can even be an expression of emotional violence, with people using the technique to drive others to the emotional breaking point. The personnel director fought his boss the only way he could handle it; he procrastinated. John and his brother (mentioned earlier) fought their father in different ways—his brother openly, John by procrastinating. John concluded his letter to me with the following insight: "Procrastination and overachieving are both reactions of hostility." Procrastination is a poor solution to a tough problem.

8

There'll Be a Way Out

A friend wrote to me:

> For me procrastination serves the very useful
> function of delaying action long enough to
> sort out the number of projects I take on com-
> pulsively. By delaying action, the number be-
> comes manageable. My tendency to operate
> from my strong sense of duty and moral obli-
> gation is thus moderated. After all, if an op-
> portunity is no longer available, I am no longer
> obligated to pursue it.

Procrastinators believe that if they wait long enough
the dreaded duties will disappear one way or another.
This is the theory of the Good Fairy: a magic wand will
pass over the task to vanish it from one's muddled mind
and busy body. Procrastinators live daily with this hope,
waiting until the last minute for the rescue operation.

Procrastinators are rescued from their oughts often
enough to perpetuate the fantasy. When procrastinators
were children, their parents ordered them to do certain
duties, like take out the garbage, or clean their room.
Then the parents reminded them time after time to do
the deed. Finally parents gave up and did it themselves.
It was easier to take out the garbage than to nag and

threaten the child into doing it. So the child learned that by waiting long enough and enduring enough nagging and empty threats one would not have to do what the authority demanded.

After procrastinators become adults, bosses, friends, and spouses rescue them often enough to perpetuate this theory. The college professor extends the term paper deadline; the boss assigns the job to another person; and, the spouse finally gives up and changes the flat tire on the car. The fallacy of the fantasy is that it's free from any consequences.

When the task refuses to go away, most procrastinators, in a frantic flurry, finish it as rapidly as possible. Some procrastinators have devised a clever way of even avoiding the day of accountability. Many people use illness to avoid deadlines and escape responsibility.

Catherine arranged for a woman to give a speech to an organization to which she belonged. When the woman did not show up, Catherine telephoned her. The woman explained, "I get deathly sick every time I eat avocados and onions. Last night I ate avocados and onions, and today I'm too sick to give the speech." The woman *chose* physical illness over fulfilling a responsibility, because illness is the perfect excuse and a logical device when one does not want to fulfill an obligation.

The price procrastinators pay for waiting for someone to rescue them is rather high. My friend concluded his letter as follows. "There is, however, a rather high price for procrastinating:

- Feeling guilty for 'putting things off.'
- Feeling guilty when people ask 'Why hasn't this project been done?'
- Losing out on opportunities and feeling in-effective, insignificant, and powerless.

54

• The feeling of worthlessness that comes from breaking promises to oneself."

When the cost of being rescued is considered, one wonders if the Good Fairy is not the devil in disguise, throwing out punctured life preservers to watch people slowly sink into senseless self-mortification. Yet, belief in the Good Fairy teases many people with the hope that someone or something will rescue them from the dreaded duty, so they wait and wait and wait until it's almost too late. Sometimes it is, much to the relief—and sadness —of the procrastinator.

Part Three

The Cure
for
Procrastination

9

STEP ONE: Analyze Your Procrastination Patterns

The first step in overcoming the problem of procrastination is to recognize and admit it as a problem.

A comparison can be drawn between the use of alcohol and the problem of procrastination. There are people who partake of alcohol on special occasions and, apparently, their indulgence does not affect their family life, social relations, or professional performance. There are other people, however, whose drinking hurts their family, friends, and job performance. Similarly, there are people who procrastinate on specific tasks on "special occasions," and their procrastinating does not significantly affect their family life, social relations, or professional performance. There are other people whose procrastinating hurts their family, friends, and job performances. Innocent bystanders suffer, and, then, both alcoholics and procrastinators hurt themselves daily.

People seemed to be helped by admitting or confessing to being procrastinators. The process was the same whether it occurred when I gave a speech or conducted a study group. First, people were embarrassed. "I've been found out," was their response. Second, after a discussion of the subject in study groups, people dropped most of their emotional defenses and felt relieved of a burden. They said, "After we started sharing our problems of procrastination, I relaxed. I didn't have to fight the problem or pretend that I liked the ways I acted." The stigma vanished, and the people lost some of their need to procrastinate. Third, after feelings of embarrassment and relief, hope emerged. People felt optimistic about being able to change.

The procrastinators believed, as most people do, that they were condemned to live and to feel and to act as they always had. Many had tried to use traditional management skills unsuccessfully. All felt trapped, handcuffed, bound by circumstances beyond their control, and guilty for not changing their ways. By understanding the causes of their procrastination and the effects of it on themselves and others, they assumed responsibility for their problems instead of blaming others. The consensus was "It's all right to *be* a procrastinator, but it's degrading to *remain* one once we know how to change."

Instant success did not follow, because most people cannot race into a new life. Most people inch their way along by moving pieces of the puzzle in place one at a time, laughing—or at least smiling—when they fall back into old procrastination patterns. A group participant expressed the process by declaring, "I'm a recovering procrastinator."

ANALYZING YOUR PROCRASTINATION PROBLEMS

After accepting procrastination as a problem, it is helpful to identify how procrastination affects us and others. The following questions may assist you in identifying your patterns of procrastination. Writing answers to the questions is usually more helpful than merely trying to sort them out in your head.

60

1. On what kind of tasks do I procrastinate? Are tasks postponed similar to one another—written work, reports, personal-conflict situations, housework, civic responsibilities, financial transactions, etc.? Are they tasks assigned by others? Are they tasks evaluated by others? Are they tasks voluntarily chosen by me? Do I procrastinate on both assigned and voluntary tasks?

2. Who is involved in my procrastination?

Employers	Friends
Employees	Teachers
Spouse	Aggressive people
Children	Passive people
Parents	Others

When procrastination always involves people in positions of authority, the pattern is clear. If procrastination occurs only in spouse-related activities, a pattern emerges that signals danger.

3. What role does each person involved play?

Rescuer	Sympathizer
Nagger	Friendly critic
Encourager	Condemner
Authority	Counselor
Praiser	Other
Empathizer	

A person may play several roles in the procrastination drama; parents may nag, rescue, praise, order, and condemn the procrastinating 30-year-old child.

After identifying patterns, procrastinators will be able to determine whether they procrastinate because they lack the information and skills to manage their time, or whether they use procrastination as a way of coping with people and responsibility. To cease procrastinating some people will need to practice skills while examining the pay-offs for their procrastination and to learn to substitute more gratifying behavior for self-defeating habits. For instance, using procrastination to express personal power and independence from the boss, spouse, parent, or teacher may be given up for the satisfaction and self-esteem received from doing a better job.

Maybe you can say with me, "I am a recovering procrastinator," and relax while you become who you want to be.

10 STEP TWO: Evict the Perfectionist

At first it seemed as if George had been stricken with a terminal case of procrastination. He postponed doing everything until someone else applied pressure. George's potential as a professional person was being sabotaged by procrastination, and this challenged my abilities and captured my imagination as I tried to help him.

For three years George and I inched our way along, with a ray of hope shining through a special report finished ahead of a deadline or a meeting conducted satisfactorily because of adequate preparation. Finally, George seemed to be in control of his life. Acting to create stimulus rather than always dashing to meet others' expectations, George celebrated victories daily rather than trudging from one brief feeling of relief to the next.

George proudly announced that he purchased his automobile license plate six weeks prior to the deadline. Six weeks and one day later a police officer stopped him for not having a new license plate on his car. When George extracted his license plate from the glove compartment of the car, the officer was not impressed and extracted a ticket from his book.

Fortunately George now had enough victories trophied in his psyche to laugh at the absurdity of this incident.

63

A year before, similar incidents provoked George to mentally and emotionally strap himself to the flogging post and beat away until he felt fatalistic about the future.

Excited about the possibility of overcoming her procrastination problem, Laura took notes in the procrastination study-group, worked hard on her priorities, and visualized herself as an efficient administrator in the organization where she worked. Her vision was clear: with the desk top clear of paper, Laura was the center of minute-by-minute executive decisions—each task handled efficiently, decisively, and wisely.

Determined to have the best priority list in the study group, Laura worked and reworked her list, knowing that when she finished it, it would be perfect. Her time chart reflected the creativity of an artist. Three colors designated the relative importance of each item. All she had to do was follow the colorful, clever plan.

Two weeks after showing her new life-plan to other group members, Laura returned to the group baffled about the plan, disappointed in herself, and deflated in spirit. The plan did not work. Interruptions evicted items of importance, and people rudely wrecked her intentions by failing to do what she expected of them. And worst of all, Laura procrastinated on several important projects, doing yellow tasks when she should have been doing brown ones. This perfect person with a perfect plan failed to perform perfectly!

The most frequent problem people had in ceasing to procrastinate related to self-expectations. Their new insights and new skills lured them to unrealistic expectations. The road to success seemed paved with perfect solutions, and the energy needed to conquer surged through these people as they anticipated a utopian existence. But when they failed to meet these expectations, their guilt feelings intensified, their despondency deepened, and their self-image sank to a new low. Their hopes of overcoming their procrastination were crushed.

Remember, it took years of mental and emotional conditioning for you to become an effective procrastinator. It will take at least a few months, if not years, to reshape the ways you relate to people and carry on your activities. Don't think that you will cease postponing tasks immediately and suddenly become a new, free, joyous person within 24 hours after reading this book. It takes time to develop the skills and to acquire the attitudes needed to become the person you want to be.

The little perfectionist inside will attempt to sabotage your efforts by whispering, "Why try? You'll never get it perfect" . . . "See, you failed. My way works best" . . . "It's not worth the effort." With a firm commitment to cease habitual procrastinating you can apply the insights and sharpen the skills described herein, evict the perfectionistic pest from its tormentor's chair, and appreciate your successes.

For the people who do not have to contend with the perfectionistic tendency, and who only need to learn and to apply skills, results will come in a relatively short time. In either case, celebrate each victory (any task completed ahead of deadline) while practicing your new attitudes and skills one day at a time.

HOW TO MANAGE CHANGE

When people decide to change behavior, two forces fight for dominance—one against change, the other for change. One side fights for the familiar and wants to keep things as they are. So some people choose to be unhappy with their old way of life rather than risking possible pain and failure by trying something different. The force for change encourages people with promises of happiness and greater success.

For procrastinators tottering between the two forces and wanting to tip the balance toward change, the following methods are suggested.

1. *Select one area or activity or task on which to practice new behavior.*

Some people discovered that by selecting one or two activities they normally procrastinate at and devising a plan for managing them on time, they began to feel better about themselves while celebrating their small victories.

Margie confessed that she felt guilty about owing letters to several friends. A simple suggestion solved her problem. She listed every person she felt guilty about not writing, scheduled one hour the following day, and wrote them. She then devised a plan to answer letters the day she received them and to do so immediately following dinner.

An executive who disliked confronting department heads scheduled executive conferences for Monday mornings. With this schedule, he visited each person every two weeks. Problems were discussed, and if nothing was urgent, the executive asked how he could assist the department head and dreamed with the person about the future. This 30 minutes every two weeks with department heads boosted morale. Emergency visits to the executive diminished because people did not have to compete for his time. The bonus for this procedure was that not every conference was filled with tension; visiting with department heads became an interesting part of the executive's job.

After failing to apply the time-management principles she knew, a student chose one term paper to finish a week ahead of the due date and did it. She celebrated for two days before the awesome truth struck; in ten days three more term papers were due in addition to finals. But she had the feel of completing something ahead of schedule, and she liked it.

Many people work their way into self-discipline one step at a time, day by day and week by week. They select a task from among those fighting for attention and schedule it. If possible, the task is placed on a routine schedule. Every day at the same time the task is given undivided attention. After that task is comfortably in place, another task is routinized, and so on until every regular responsibility and task has found its place. Taming one task or responsibility at a time gradually changes behavior, and the feelings of failure and despair are replaced by victory, confidence, and hope.

2. *Reward yourself for performing properly.*

When faced with a difficult or time-consuming task, some people find it helpful to establish a self-reward system.

John, the minister of a local congregation, used this method to round up a repeating responsibility. Eleven o'clock Sunday morning happened every week whether John was ready to preach or not. Yet week after week John was still writing Sunday's sermon at Saturday midnight or even seven o'clock Sunday morning. Then John decided that Saturday noon was the deadline for sermon preparation, and if he completed writing the sermon on schedule, he could watch the sports programs on television Saturday afternoon.

A self-reward system is an extra inducement to do what you can with the time available, to shrug off the fear of failure, and to assume responsibility for your actions.

3. *Contract for a procrastination partner.*

Some people need the support of another person while they attempt to change. These people agree to report to another person once or twice a week. The agreement serves two purposes: 1) procrastinators tell the partners their past actions and intentions—what activities were and are planned; 2) procrastinators report the problems and victories they are having with procrastination.

To be helpful partners avoid 1) playing critical parent —they refuse to "fuss" at procrastinators for failing to fulfill promises to themselves, and 2) playing sympathetic parent—"you poor child, those other people are being naughty to you for giving you so much work." The partner 1) compliments for achievements, and 2) gives feedback objectively, including offering suggestions for overcoming procrastination.

The partner program is another way procrastinators take charge of their lives by establishing their *own* base of accountability.

4. *Picture the product.*

If you have been conditioned to look for mistakes, incompetency, incompleteness, and tardiness, that is what you see. People who visualize themselves procrastinating anticipate frantic last-minute activity, feelings of frustration, and dissatisfaction with their efforts. The picture becomes firmly fixed in the mind. By anticipating inadequate performance and negative feelings, they get what they expect.

One thing essential in overcoming procrastination is to wedge the failure picture out of the mind with a success picture of performance and feelings. This method was resisted by several people working on the problem of procrastination. They resisted change because they could not or would not visualize themselves as efficient people. After some probing, I discovered that their resistance derived from their unpleasant associations with efficient people. They did not like efficient people, because efficient people were "self-righteous, emotionally cold computers." While trying to visualize themselves as nonprocrastinators, they saw themselves becoming "self-righteous, emotionally cold computers," and they preferred their present "human" way of relating to others.

Others rebelled against visualizing themselves as efficient because they did not want to live under the pressure of *always* being efficient—which meant being perfect and never procrastinating on anything.

Visualizing success does not assume perfection or any specific way of relating to people. Recovering procrastinators can continue to be charming and sensitive to others even while doing what they have agreed to do.

In *People at Work* Dave Francis and Mike Woodcock express the challenge succinctly:

> A need for change must be felt by a person before there is much of a possibility that something will actually be done. Development also requires having a mental picture of how things will look when they are better. We need to visualize the final objective in terms that make sense to us.

Creating a mental picture of how things will look is half of self-imaging. When using this method, we need also to imagine our *feelings* in the situation, to see and to plan for particular feelings. This happens in an almost unconscious way with everyone. We think about visiting someone we resent and *anticipate* being nervous, secretly angry, and uptight. In a way, we visualize the feelings. We think about a very difficult task and feel either excitedly challenged or filled with dread.

Art resented his district manager's authoritarian insensitive way of relating to field representatives. When Art anticipated a conference with the manager, he did not sleep well the night before. Awakening the next morning,

69

he was irritable at home and greeted his secretary with a gruff "Morning." Because he anticipated (visualized) the boss's orders and criticism, Art was angry and resentful before the conference began. In essence, he planned how he would act and feel in the conference.

With a little help in picturing himself successful in conferences with the manager, Art changed the way he acted and felt in the situation. Prior to the weekly conference, Art imagined himself feeling calm and confident, listening to the manager with interest, and reporting and responding objectively. Art pictured the scene several times before going into the conference. In a few months Art became the calm, confident person he visualized himself to be. Thinking and feelings followed behavior.

Several people discovered that by visualizing themselves handling tasks more efficiently and feeling confident while doing so, they became the persons they visualized. These people began to assume success instead of failure, and anticipating success generated the interest and energy to become the persons they chose to be.

PROBLEMS ALONG THE WAY

Changing the ways one relates to people and manages tasks can cause problems. After procrastinating for years, people who cease often disrupt the systems in which they live and work. Other people in these systems know what to expect from procrastinators and those close to procrastinators usually receive some satisfaction from playing the heavy roles in the procrastinators' drama. An abrupt change in behavior sometimes jars personal relations. If a procrastinator is married to a spouse who needs to play parent, and suddenly the procrastinator becomes a responsible person, the spouse is stuck with an outdated

70

vocabulary—"Why don't you . . . ," "When are you going to . . . ," "It's time for you to . . . ," "If I've told you once, I've told you a hundred times. . . ."

When dealing with reformed procrastinators, executives, managers, and supervisors may be overloaded with blank memo pads and begin to feel useless without someone to rescue and to remind and remind and remind.

There is another reason for procrastinators not to become responsible too quickly; they may irritate others with their self-righteousness. There is nothing more irritating than people who are always efficient, especially if these people are reformed procrastinators.

However, there is not much to worry about, for we procrastinators rarely succeed in changing our procrastination patterns all at once. Gradual change is probably more helpful for all concerned

Overcoming procrastination can be viewed as a process to be lived through with increasing satisfaction as you decide who you want to become, how you want to act, and how you want to feel.

Remember: Procrastination is learned behavior. You can unlearn it, and you can learn new ways of acting that will make your life happier and more effective. Choose one area or task and work on that, using the techniques outlined in this chapter. Change may not come overnight, but it will come.

11

STEP THREE:
Clarify Your Values

In the fight for survival or success, procrastinators and perfectionists often lose sight of what they believe. Jim confessed, "At age 36 I have reached my goals of being rich and being my own boss. I own the company, but I hurt a lot of people doing it, and I really feel guilty about that. I guess I lost something along the way. I wonder if it's worth it."

Conflict between what procrastinators believe and what they do or fail to do causes disappointment in themselves and a resulting low self-image. No less a person than the apostle Paul confessed to this problem. "I cannot understand my own actions, I do not act as I want to act; on the contrary, I do what I detest. . . . Miserable wretch that I am! Who will save me from this body of death" (Romans 7:15-16, 24 Moffatt). Paul fought the battle between what he believed and how he acted. In contemporary terms, Paul's problem is called a value crisis.

If what we believed directed what we did and what we did reflected what we believed, there would be no conflict, but life is not that simple. We often have a conflict of two important values. Procrastinators respond to pseudo-emergencies instead of considering the relative value of the act or task. A day, a week, a year, or 20 years later they sit with Jim, wondering if it was worth it.

72

WHAT DO I EXPECT,
WHAT DO THEY EXPECT?

The conflict between intention and action is intensified when there is a difference between what we expect of ourselves and what others expect of us. We live in a less-than-perfect environment where others expect us to think, feel, and act in particular ways and do not always live up to our expectations. To survive satisfactorily we accept life as it is, which includes considering others' expectations of us. We have to accept life as it is before we can make it what it can be.

The conflict between our own expectations and those of others can cause frustration in our ways of relating to people and managing tasks. Some people live more by what others expect them to do and be than by what they expect of themselves.

Clergy are often caught in this dilemma. While proclaiming the importance of spending time with one's spouse and children, they may neglect their own families because other people "need their pastor." Parishioners expect their pastor to be available at all times. This is not simply a time-management problem; it is a value crisis.

Mary, a 35-year-old mother of four, thought there might be a connection between her dirty house and her mother's constant nagging. She said, "I don't clean the house sufficiently when mother comes to visit, and it really irritates her. As soon as she walks in the door, she surveys the scene to see what must be done immediately to make the house livable. Her whole week's visit is spoiled by her straightening closets, washing woodwork, and dusting everything in sight. My husband told me he was afraid that any minute she would grab him, rip his clothes off, push him in the shower, and start scrubbing."

"What do you say to her?" I asked.

"I leave her alone rather than fight over it as I used to. A clean house is the most important thing in her life. I grew up in a home where people were reluctant to sit on the furniture for fear of soiling it."

"Doesn't it make you angry to have your mother take over your house?" I asked.

"A little at times, but I know I'll have the last word," Mary said.

"How?"

"Last week after packing her suitcase, she inspected the house, admired her work, put on her coat, and started out the door. 'Now your house is lovely,' she assured me.

"I replied, 'It does look like a museum, but don't worry about it, Mother. It will look terrible in three days.' You should have seen the look on her face. I hate to admit it, but it felt good seeing her disappointed."

"What do you have against a clean house?" I asked.

"Nothing. I want my house to look just like it did when mother left, but I can't seem to get around to it with everything else I have to do."

A spotless house was extremely important to Mary's mother—one of her highest values. Mary also believed that an orderly, clean house was important, yet not important enough to do much about it. Rebelling against her mother and her spotless-house value, she felt guilty about her negligence. Wisely she had *decided* that time with her husband and children was more important than spending eight hours a day dusting, vacuuming, and straightening the house. The decision did not automatically evict the guilt associated with a less-than-spotless house. The values caught early in life are not easily exorcized, even after we intellectually decide they are not valid for us.

CLARIFYING YOUR VALUES

To maintain a creative, constructive life we must remain in control of those parts of life we can do something about. There are some things we cannot control—a heart attack takes someone from us, the economy kicks us out of a job, a tornado rips our home to shreds. In such traumatic situations we respond the best we can with the best we have. We cannot control others' opinions or feelings; we can control *how we respond to others*. We can control our time and attitude toward life.

The foundation for overcoming procrastination and developing a new way of managing tasks and relating to people is a firm mental and emotional grip on our values. Assuming responsibility for yourself involves identifying and choosing your values, instead of mechanically complying with or rebelling against values caught early in life. A way to do this is to identify the values that affect our feelings and actions, and then examine them. To assist in this process a short list of value areas follows to stimulate your thinking. After reviewing the areas, list the ten most important values in your life, ranking them in the order of importance.

The most important things in my life are:

- Family values (financial security for my family; making my spouse happy; rearing my children to become responsible, happy people; creating an intimate marriage)
- Professional success
- Being thought of as a friendly person
- Having people like me
- Keeping an orderly, clean house
- Owning a large home
- Being fair with others
- Influencing others (personal power)

- Being on time for appointments
- Physical health
- Being loyal to people
- Recreation
- Hobbies
- Money
- Being independent
- Prestige
- Serving others (being needed)
- Practicing my religion (attending worship services, giving money, helping others, serving on committees, social justice, prayer)
- Others

After listing ten values in the order of their importance, examine them by answering the following questions for each one.

1. Where did I get this value? Parents, teachers, church, peers, reading, television, etc.?

2. Is the value *still* important to me?

3. Am I living as if I believe in this value? If so, why? If not, why not?

4. Does the value reflect what I believe or what I think I *ought* to believe?

5. Have I affirmed this value consciously or am I just parroting the past?

After examining the ten values, select the five most important ones and place the values on a card or sheet of paper to be used as a reminder of who you are and who you want to become. Review the values regularly, because they become the guiding principles for making decisions.

For instance, if you place a high value on family life and believe it is important to devote quality time with each child, when a job is offered that requires three-week trips away from home and pays $5000 a year increase in salary, you will have a basis for deciding before accepting or rejecting it. However, if you rank money high because of what it gives (power, prestige, house, luxuries), then you may decide to take the new job despite the inner tension and family conflict it could cause. Most people experience these conflicts, but they just do it unconsciously. As a result, some people are lured into situations by the excitement of the moment instead of considering the costs and rewards of their decision. These same principles hold for inner-office decisions and parent-child relations.

Because most people's values change from time to time, it is helpful to examine values every year or two to determine whether it is time to have a "garage sale" of antiquated ideas and unusable values.

A DAILY DISCIPLINE

The preceding plan will help many people, yet many of us need specific procedures to help us live what we believe, especially when daily pressures tempt us to compromise. More than 20 years ago I was forced to establish specific procedures for managing life.

As a 26-year-old executive with a compulsive drive to succeed, I began having stomach pains. The physician said, "Loren, unless you change either your schedule or your attitude, you will have ulcers in two years."

"How do I change?" I asked.

"I don't have the slightest idea, but you had better do it or it's going to be a painful climb to the top," the doctor replied.

After analyzing both my activities and attitudes, I established two life-saving principles.

First, I resolved not to have lunch or dinner with anyone I did not like if I could avoid it. Lunch became a leisurely visit with friends and food, instead of an intense encounter with clients.

Second, I resolved to begin each day in a relaxed meditation instead of bouncing out of bed in a sprinter's pace. Arising 30 minutes earlier than necessary enabled me to choose the way I would be that day.

Christian meditation is one way we can keep our values in our actions. In his book, *Taste and See*, William Paulsell writes, "Our devotional lives and our spiritual experiences are intimately related to our jobs, our families, and our community life. We do not have to make a connection between our spirituality and our lives in the world. It is already there."

To receive full benefit from the integration of our attitudes and daily actions we need daily discipline. You may find the following procedures helpful.

First, begin the day by listening to your inner voice. While sitting in my lounge chair staring out the window, thoughts stroll across my mental screen—pressing problems, yesterday's victories, special people doing special things, and lively opportunities appear to be considered. A prayer of offering and thanksgiving to God places the thoughts in proper perspective and releases the mind's grip on them.

Second, review the day's activities and anticipate the irritating interruptions. Many people pray, mentioning each person and activity while asking for guidance and a Christian spirit in carrying out the daily tasks.

Third, review your values. On the wall in my study, where I begin the day, are reminders of who I am. Two pictures of Jesus, one laughing and one serious, and photographs of my family remind me who loves and needs me and whom I love and need. A court jester painted by a special friend keeps telling me that I need to laugh at myself when I make mistakes, especially when I am taking myself too seriously. The words "Unless you love someone nothing makes sense" are on a banner which I face as I meditate.

Fourth, set your emotional tone for the day. Decide how you want to feel as well as act. I enjoy beginning the day relaxed, anticipating some exciting problems and people.

Fifth, relax and listen. Thomas Merton wrote, "Often meditation will yield insights that are deeply practical, almost mundane."

For me, Christian meditation is the basic ingredient for a creative, exciting day of tackling tough tasks, ordering easy oughts about, and dealing with interruptions that sometimes turn out to be extraordinary opportunities.

In *Christian Unity: Matrix for Mission,* Paul A. Crow Jr. wrote, "Contemplation—intense prayer, meditation, spiritual reflection, solitude—is available to every Christian and is your and my calling. Indeed it is part of our salvation from the frantic pace of modern life, which drains our spirits in countless ways."

William Paulsell captures the thesis when he writes, "As far as life in the spirit is concerned, the denial we must practice in these modern times involves the use of our time. In order to develop a deep spiritual life we must give up time normally used for other things and use it for prayer. Making good use of time is a modern form of Christian asceticism."

Keeping our values straight is the biggest challenge we face each day. We need all the help we can get.

12

STEP FOUR:
Set Realistic Goals

"What do you want to be when you grow up?" a visitor in our home asked Mark, who was ten years old at the time.

"A brain surgeon or a fireman," Mark quickly replied.

Children dream goals early in life, yet are not expected to do anything about them yet. Though modified slightly, the same problem haunts some procrastinators. They have a vague, idealized picture of "what they want to be when they grow up," but do not know exactly how they will achieve that picture.

SETTING GOALS

Recovering procrastinators set goals for themselves and devise plans for reaching those goals. We need to know *what* we want to accomplish so we can plan *how* we will accomplish it. Being president of the firm or an outstanding teacher, owning a beautiful seaside home, making Phi Beta Kappa, playing professional baseball, winning the Boston Marathon are colorful ideals that need plans to become realities.

Yet, overwhelmed with yesterday's undone deeds and today's oughts, procrastinators seldom get much beyond the fantasy stage and fail to plan *specifically* how they will attain their goals. Many people seem to think that if they work hard and keep busy someone will reward them with whatever they wish for. To use *wisely* our energy and ability is to choose goals carefully and to devise methods for achieving the goals.

The first step in the process is to write down your one-year, five-year, and ten-year goals. My procrastination study groups found goal-setting to be the most helpful aid in overcoming procrastination, the foundation for everything else needed. *Don't short-cut the process.* Write out your goals carefully.

Following are goals some seminar participants wrote:

- To establish my own plumbing business in five years.
- To start a consulting firm to help organizations write effective business letters when I retire.
- To compliment employees, verbally and in writing, when performance warrants.
- To be vice-president of a firm by age 38.
- To spend an hour a day talking with my spouse.
- To play with my children every day.
- To set aside one hour a day to plan for the future.
- To plan next week's work the preceding Friday.
- To walk two miles a day for health's sake.
- To begin each day with 30 minutes of devotional time.

Use the bits-vs-blitz method for managing big goals and tasks. Subdivide big and long range goals into subgoals. When viewed in one lump, goals have a way of discouraging us, so they need to be cut down to manageable size. You do not decide to save $10,000 without a method for doing so. You usually decide to save $25 or $100 a month for a certain number of years. Each month the subgoals are reached with a feeling of accomplishment. This principle applies to any big goal. Authors do not write books; they write words, sentences, paragraphs, and pages.

Martha used the bits-vs-blitz method to get rid of the "Housemaid Blues." Her goal was to keep the house reasonably arranged and clean. She used to think about making beds, dusting, vacuuming, hanging up clothes, washing and drying clothes, cleaning bathrooms, and preparing meals, and got tired just thinking about it. Then she subgoaled, and now no longer thinks in terms of cleaning the whole house. She assigns herself a room or two or a combination of chores. When she finishes today's assignment, she celebrates without feeling guilty about other unfinished chores.

Whether our goal involves recurring responsibilities, as did Martha's, or whether it entails a steady climb to conquer it once-and-for-all, it is helpful to have subgoals to give us a taste of achievement and to maintain our interest and enthusiasm.

EVALUATING GOALS

Answering the following questions will assist in deciding whether or not to pursue the goals.

1. *Is this goal realistic?* For me the goal of becoming president of my alma mater is unrealistic for several reasons: my lack of appropriate credentials, my deficiency of political skills, and a dislike of most of the work university presidents do.

2. *What is required to accomplish this goal?* Write each phase of the process it will take to accomplish the goal. In deciding whether to write a book on procrasti-

nation, I identified the steps in the process. They included researching written material, enlisting people to interview, interviewing them, writing notes, studying notes, discovering solutions to procrastination, testing the solutions, outlining the book, writing the book, finding a publisher, and so on.

3. *How much time will be required to accomplish this goal?* After listing the tasks required to write a book on procrastination, I had to decide if I had the time to do it and if I *wanted* to give the time to write it. I had to decide whether writing the book was more important than some other things I wanted to do. In deciding to write the book, I decided *not* to do some things, for I did not have time to do everything I wanted to.

After estimating the time to reach each goal, determine whether it is more important than other things you want or need to do. This is crucial in goal setting, especially for procrastinators, because they have a tendency to stuff goals on top of goals. When trying to accomplish too many goals at once, people seldom satisfy themselves with any of them.

4. *Do I have the ability to accomplish this goal?* Many procrastinators are reluctant to admit their limitations. Though it is not disgraceful to be deficient in certain skills, procrastinators often assume they *should* be able to do more than they can. When you set goals, it is helpful to assess your abilities. Make two lists. With one list describe your skills—what you do well. On the other list describe what you don't do well. If the goal requires skills that you do not have, decide whether to learn the needed skill or to abandon the goal.

5. *Will the goal help me feel the way I want to feel?* A goal should affirm or increase one's self-esteem and satisfaction in living. This is not to suggest a selfish or self-centered approach to life; people who live the self-

83

centered life eventually become disgusted with themselves. Relating to others responsibly increases our self-respect and causes us to feel good about ourselves.

6. *How does working for and reaching this goal affect other significant people in my life?* If you work 18 hours a day to become president of the firm, while ignoring your family, your spouse and children may feel abandoned, despite the higher income you are earning.

7. *What is the cost of this goal mentally, emotionally, physically, and spiritually?* Often the cost of big goals is more than first appears in terms of stress, lost friends and family, physical health, and spiritual deterioration. Sometimes the cost is worth the goal in terms of less strain on the budget, more intimate family relations, and increased self-confidence. We should calculate the cost before buying the ticket for the trip.

8. *How does this goal support and reflect my values?* People can get so caught up in the excitement of challenging goals that they sacrifice their values to reach their goals. A worthy goal attained by unworthy means is an internal disaster that eats away at a person's emotional, physical, and spiritual being.

REVIEW YOUR GOALS

Writing goals does not commit us to embrace them tenaciously for the remainder of our lives. Our goals will probably change with additional achievement, wider experience, and changing circumstances. But for now, set the goals, examine them, choose the ones you want to reach, and plan the methods for accomplishing them.

Review your goals regularly. Doing so reminds us of why we put up with those boring chores and irritating people, and it may give us a hint of why they put up with

us. By regularly reviewing our goals we keep them before us, and this helps us to keep moving in the direction
we have chosen.

13 STEP FIVE: Fight Frustration with Effective Scheduling

Peter Drucker, an authority on business management, wrote, "Executives are forever being exhorted to plan their work. This sounds imminently plausible—the only thing wrong with it is that it rarely works. The plans tend to remain on paper, tend to remain good intentions." Some people are excellent planners, but poor implementers. Nothing significant happens until we decide *when* we will do what. Once that decision is made, we are free to do today's work *if* we learn to keep promises to ourselves.

Once we decide to act and determine when we are going to do what and can be assured that we will fulfill our self-commitment, then, and only then, will our minds and emotions be free to concentrate on what we want and need to do *now*, systematically taking each task in its turn.

USING CALENDARS

Frustration is eased by giving each goal, objective, and task a place and time on the calendar. During the past 30 years I have discovered that I need three types of calendars to control time and tasks. Others may need more or less calendaring to control their living.

1. A *yearly calendar* records major goals and tasks. It assists in distributing major responsibilities and gives an

overview of living. The calendar not only records the due date; it also marks preparation time in anticipation of the due date. For instance, I agreed in October to give three lectures May 15. Three dates were placed on the calendar. April 2 marked preparation time for lectures. May 1 signaled final drafts for lectures. Recording preparation time is essential to staying in control of major responsibilities.

You should regularly review your calendar. If you do not review it, you may agree to a major responsibility six months hence when you already have three such responsibilities within a three-week period. We need to know what is "coming down the pike" to make decisions today. Every person has special times of the year that require special preparation and can be anticipated. The yearly calendar records major responsibilities and intermediate dates for planning and preparation.

2. A *quarterly calendar* records intermediate steps needed to achieve major goals and tasks. The three lectures in May required additional deadlines on the quarterly calendar: April 5—complete the first draft of the first lecture; April 12—complete the first draft of the second lecture; April 20—complete the first draft of the third lecture. Establishing intermediate objectives relieves the frustration we anticipate from having to do a big job.

3. A *weekly calendar* records living patterns. The weekly calendar is scheduled with energy levels, job demands, personal preferences, and family in mind. Some daily and weekly responsibilities demand their time on the schedule.

Schedule routine tasks and recurring responsibilities the same time each day or week. This conserves energy (routine tasks are usually scheduled for low-energy times) and eliminates some of the dread associated with knowing that eventually the tasks will have to be done.

Boring tasks are easier to take in small doses. When working in educational administration, primarily seeking funds for Lexington Theological Seminary, I waited until I returned from a trip to write the reports of my visits. While I enjoyed discussing the seminary with people, I despised writing those reports; it usually took eight to ten hours after each trip. I dreaded it so much I did something about it. While on a trip, I forced myself to write the reports and letters generated by the day's work each evening in the motel. I still disliked the chore, but it was more palatable when taken in smaller doses. Scheduling boring and toilsome tasks daily eliminates the temptation to postpone them to a more "convenient" time.

Difficult tasks require a special enforcer to prompt procrastinators to tackle them. People respond to difficult tasks differently. Willard Wickizer, an executive, jumps on tough tasks first thing in the morning. "My day begins with the most difficult task I have to do. I can't concentrate on anything else until I get rid of it. And when I finish it, I coast through the rest of the day clicking off easier duties. I need the stimulation from a big victory to stimulate me for the day's work."

Other people use the opposite approach. They need to work through the easy oughts to the difficult task. The easy oughts distract them, and they like to accomplish several easy oughts to build a feeling of accomplishment. This approach generates the energy to take on the big tasks, the way kindling sparks an open fire until enough heat is generated to ignite the big log.

SCHEDULING MAKE-UP TIME

In using a weekly calendar, be sure to plan for the unexpected. A weekly calendar without methods for managing the unexpected creates more frustration than it eliminates. Two devices are essential for weekly calendaring:

1. *Plan make-up time each day.* Make-up time enables one to handle interruptions with single-mindedness. When I was serving as pastor of a church, interruptions always generated much inner tension. I would be writing a congregational letter, or studying the Scriptures, or planning a special program, and a knock on the door would produce a troubled parishioner. The parishioner would pour his or her heart out over family or financial problems. While trying to listen, I could never completely dismiss the half-done task and, as a result, I was only half present, intellectually and emotionally, when I was needed the most. After I placed make-up time in my schedule, I could relax, listen, and be totally present to the person. I knew *when* I would complete the half-done task.

2. *Plan make-up time at the end of the week (or work period).* Some days unexpected events outnumber planned activities and the daily make-up time falls short of its purpose. Tasks that should be completed this week but not today need a place in the schedule. Three hours of make-up time Friday afternoon saved my sanity. It is used for two purposes. First, it is a time slot into which I place undone deeds that were evicted from their neat place in the line-up too late to make the daily make-up time. Second, if by chance, hard work, and wise scheduling I keep faith with the week's schedule, I reward myself with three hours of recreation.

The key to using make-up time effectively is to reschedule tasks at specific times in the make-up time slots. Otherwise, we operate under the illusion that anything and everything can be made up later, and we are back to the procrastinator's pattern.

KEEPING A TIME LOG

In preparation for using a detailed weekly calendar some people discover that they need to identify what they are doing with their time and energy before they decide what they want to do. Keeping a log of activities for a few weeks helps them identify the patterns of their working and living habits.

Ann Allison, an administrative assistant in the Graduate Educational Program of the College of Nursing at the University of Kentucky, assisted professors, dealt with students, and processed hundreds of documents. Interruptions were constant. While she was trying to complete all her must tasks, student after student approached her for information and help in filling out forms. The telephone rang regularly. Being a conscientious person, Ann was concerned about students and wanted to get all the work completed every day. When she couldn't, she often took work home.

In an attempt to get a better grip on the unruly work load, she developed a form and kept a log. The form follows, as an example, with only a few of the scores of tasks she recorded.

	Monday	Tuesday	Wednesday	Thursday	Friday	Weekly Total
Phone calls Incoming						
Phone calls Outgoing						
Person-to-Person Contact: Students						
Person-to-Person Contact: Inquirers						
Person-to-Person Contact: Faculty						

Keeping a log gives an overview of how one is using time. Some people discover they are trying to or are expected to do more than any one person can. For others this process is shocking because they discover that they are not using their time wisely; they are wasting a great deal of time on insignificant activities and neglecting more important responsibilities. A log identifies what we are doing so we can decide what we want to do.

14 STEP SIX: Make Effective Use of a To Do List

With hostility oozing between the words, John said, "I would like to write down 20 things to do—and not do a single one of them." In recent years the To Do List has taken on a charismatic quality; some people proclaim its saving grace, others denounce its demonic influence.

The wife of a professor of business administration agreed with John, "If I hear one more word about a To Do List I think I'll scream."

"All To Do Lists do is to make me feel guilty for not doing what I intended," complained Carl.

One member of a procrastination study group was adamant about not writing a list of intentions. She complained that the list did not help her get any more done and only made her feel guilty. She described the list as a warden of her conscience; once she wrote tasks down she was committed to do them. The advantage of not making a list, she contended, was that she was then not bound by her intentions. "And furthermore," she rationalized, "if I don't write them down, I can forget about them for a while, and then they don't bother me."

"Not me," I quickly replied. "A task refuses to leave me alone until I write it down and decide *when* I will do it. Don't those tasks sneak into your mind when you are trying to do something else? For instance, once I decide that the house needs painting, every television commercial on house improvement and paint pricks my conscience. Newspaper ads and people painting their houses remind me of my negligence. Once I `accept the claim of any ought, big or small, it haunts me until I give it proper attention or decide it's not worth doing."

She replied, "It affects me the same way, but I still hate To Do Lists—and I'm not convinced."

To Do Lists serve us well *if* we use them effectively and understand how they help us attain our goals. Our aim is to gain more control over our own lives. For example:

- Instead of automatically reacting to an authority (boss, spouse, etc.), we *choose* to act a particular way. When the authority makes demands on us, we consciously decide what we will or will not do, without being unduly upset.
- Instead of begging for affection or praise or punishment from others, which causes us to say yes too much, we politely explain why we will or will not do the deed requested.
- Instead of waiting for the pressure of a deadline, we apply our own pressure. We set our deadlines ahead of the deadlines set by authority figures, and we keep them. We report to ourselves before we report to others.
- Instead of being primarily other-directed, we become inner-motivated, because we know the kind of person we want to become and the goals we are striving to achieve.
- Instead of perceiving To Do Lists as standing in judgment over us, we use them as servants to be ordered about, altered as necessary, and admired when appropriate.

Some procrastinators will be tempted to put off making a To Do List because of their tendency to avoid evaluation. Others may assure themselves that they are too busy to take the time to plan. Herman Krannear, board chairman of Inland Container Corporation, observed:

> When I hear a man talk about how hard he works, and how seldom he sees his family, I am almost certain that this man will not succeed in the creative aspects of business . . . and most of the important things that have to be done are the results of creative acts.

Being too busy to plan assures half-results and possible failure, whether the person is a coach of a football team, a business executive, the president of a university, a parent of four children, a homemaker, or a teacher of first-grade children. Management consultant R. Alec MacKenzie succinctly captures the idea in a few words, "While planning requires time, in the end it saves time and gets better results."

Procrastinators will have to fight for the time to plan and to make To Do Lists, because their present ways of coping have rewards that depend on their not getting things done on time or accomplishing with less than total effort. After making To Do Lists, procrastinators will have to fight the tendency to feel defeated because they do not complete the scores of tasks they plan with their unrealistic visions of themselves.

HOW TO USE A TO DO LIST

If applied, the following principles of To Do Lists will reward us with results.

1. *Transfer the weekly scheduled items to a daily*

To Do List. At the beginning of the week, review the week's activities and decide which days you will do specific difficult tasks. To load Monday with all the time- and-energy consuming tasks is to invite defeat.

2. *Record the routine tasks.*

3. *Determine the priority of each task.* While time-management experts disagree on many things, they agree that tasks need to be listed in order of their importance. This is especially important for procrastinators who tend to avoid tough tasks by fiddling with easy ones.

Use two symbols to designate priorities. *M* is for *Must* tasks which must be completed today. *Must* tasks include tasks with deadlines established by circumstances: a report is due at five or tomorrow is Christmas. Most days should include some time for creative thinking and problem solving instead of being suffocated with emergency management activity. This is the type of activity that is neglected and often evicted from the To Do List because it does not *feel* urgent. To Do Lists include *Must* time to reflect, brood, and toy with long-range goals and next week's speech.

C is for *Could* tasks which can be completed today, but do not have to be. *Could* tasks often fill the time gaps when we get frustrated with difficult tasks, or have ten minutes between conferences, or when all *Must* tasks are completed.

4. *After designating M and C tasks, arrange them in the order of their importance.*

Must Tasks	Could Tasks
1.	1.
2.	2.
3.	3.

5. *To alert yourself to tasks on which you are most likely to procrastinate, identify tasks by three symbols:* $R =$ Routine tasks; $W =$ Want to tasks, special challenges we enjoy, recreation, and family activities; $D =$ Difficult and disliked tasks. R and D tasks require special attention because they are the ones that usually get shelved. If your To Do List does not include some W's, it is time to evaluate your attitude, your work and play habits, and your place of employment.

6. *Estimate the time each task will take or the time to be given to it today; then add up the total hours.* Include make-up time. In *Getting Things Done*, Edwin C. Bliss writes:

> Avoid thinking in terms of "working on it for an hour or so." Instead, assign yourself the task of completing the outline or finishing the research or writing the introduction. Then, when you have done so, you will be able to put it aside with a feeling of having accomplished something specific and with a clear idea of what the next step will be.

This is good advice for people with tidy minds who are comfortable disciplining themselves. But if procrastinators follow this advice, they might spend the entire day on the first *Must* task. With visions of a *perfect* introduction that will hypnotize the audience, they might nurse the task to death while the hours fly by.

Recovering procrastinators start tasks ahead of deadlines to eliminate outside pressure and last-minute frustration and to produce a better product. By working an hour on a speech, jotting notes, rearranging ideas, and experimenting with the language, you can gain a feeling of achievement in a relaxed atmosphere while avoiding unrealistic perfectionism.

96

By estimating the time each task will take, we not only decide the energy and time it deserves in our busy lives, we avoid overscheduling ourselves, which is a temptation of procrastinators. From time to time we will overestimate and underestimate time needs. If necessary, we reschedule some tasks for another day instead of wallowing in feelings of failure. However, if a task appears on your To Do List three times without any attention, either do it, or forget it, or reschedule it for a less busy time. A deadline may be extended *once,* and in extreme cases *twice,* but if deadlines are extended too often, we are either failing to plan effectively or are slipping back into "If I had more time. . . ."

7. *Evaluate at the close of the day and prepare for tomorrow.* I prefer to jot down the next day's agenda at the close of the work day and examine it the first thing the next day. Some people prefer to begin the day making their To Do List; it gives them a feeling of accomplishment just to list and arrange the tasks.

8. *Schedule when what tasks will be done. This involves four things:*

Assess as accurately as possible your capacity for work. In *How to Enjoy Work and Get More Fun Out of Life,* O. A. Battista says, "No two people possess the same work capacity, just as no two people have identical fingerprints, or equivalent appetites. To *enjoy* your work you must learn the best pace at which your body will operate." Procrastinators are forever comparing themselves to other people, and thus are often competing without openly entering the contest. Couple this with a reluctance to admit limitations, and procrastinators set a standard that may be totally unrealistic without ever considering their capacity for work. Energy output, the amount of energy we have to use in doing, is affected by attitudes toward work, basic metabolism, physical fitness, and self-image. For scores of reasons each person has his or her own capacity for work and play. By assessing our energy levels we can more accurately plan how much work can be accomplished in a given period of time.

Identify the time of day when energy is high and when it is low. Are you a morning or evening person? Some people are more alert mentally in the morning, others need half a day to get the juices flowing. Some people schedule creative tasks in the afternoon, others find that after lunch it's all downhill.

After identifying energy levels, *schedule regular tasks that warrant routine effort during low-energy times and difficult tasks that demand your best during high-energy times.* Alan Lakein, a management expert, says "Trying to do the same thing at the same time each day both conserves and generates energy." This practice sets a pattern for people who tend to procrastinate on routine tasks and avoid difficult ones.

Assess the best time for private time and people time. Being a slow starter, I prefer private time first thing in the morning to get organized and to place problems in my mind so that the unconscious will work on them while I attend to other matters. After deciding what I am going to do, I am ready for people, conferences, classes, and meetings. For me 10 P.M. to 2 A.M. is creative time. Telephones stop ringing, people go to bed, and four hours of relative silence assures the mind that it will be uninterrupted. Other people are zombies after 9 P.M. and lively at 8 A.M.

Scheduling work and play is a personal matter that is affected by many things, and each person needs to decide and to design the methods most helpful to him or her. Knowing when and how we do what best is basic to getting control of our lives. When attacking the problem of procrastination, we are doing more than attempt-

98

ing to change habituated responses to people, events, and activities; we are trying to change our attitudes toward people, work, play, and self.

A word of caution to procrastinators. After some recovering procrastinators learn to organize their living, they fall in love with their organizational charts, To Do Lists, and clever procedures. Too much organization creates as much waste and confusion as too little organization. Design the organization you need when you need to, and eliminate unnecessary organization when it outlives its usefulness.

15 STEP SEVEN: Don't Gift Wrap the Garbage

Our neighbor's garbage can glistened like a china plate, and the contents were packaged for display in Saks Fifth Avenue; she gift wrapped her garbage. Whether she was a compulsive cleaner or merely concerned about the sanitation workers' opinions of her, I don't know. Fortunately we moved before I sneaked next door in the middle of the night to steal and inspect her garbage.

Because of their propensity for perfection, procrastinators often gift wrap the "garbage" duties of their lives; the least important tasks often get the most time and energy. Fiddling with routine tasks or insignificant oughts and trying to do them perfectly, procrastinators often exhaust themselves on tasks that could be accomplished with leftover energy.

Well-meaning parents and misguided writers brainwash people to perform all tasks equally well. One author advises: "Determine to give your best to every job, large and small." Giving your best to every job, large or small, is self-defeating, because there are jobs and chores worth doing that do not require more than a second of thought and an ounce of energy. It is not necessary to gift wrap the garbage to get the job done. Gift wrapping the garbage is ironing socks, rewriting a routine letter to a relative three times, giving four reasons in writing why you can't give a speech to the Rotary Club, and sending three perfectly worded memos to the same person requesting the same information which could have been secured by a 30-second telephone call.

When we gift wrap the garbage duties, the more important tasks do not get the time and energy they deserve because the deadline is on us. One time-management expert warns, "Perfectionism is a disease, because it goes beyond what is *needed*. To obtain the first 90 percent toward perfectionism is usually easy. The last five percent is usually extremely costly—watch for the perfectionists of this life, and watch out for yourself if you tend to be one." The author is correct in principle, but has the five percent on the wrong end of the task. For most perfectionists and procrastinators devote 90 percent of their energy and thinking to the first five percent of the task and, because of the lack of time, give five percent of their effort to the last 90 percent of the task. Trying to perfect the first five percent frustrates and defeats them; the first sentence has to be perfect before the remainder of the report or letter or speech can be written.

PRINCIPLES FOR RECOVERING PROCRASTINATORS

1. *Recovering procrastinators decide what is worth doing adequately and which tasks deserve best effort and then act accordingly.* They acknowledge that almost everything they do could be improved with more time, more thinking, and more effort. When overwhelmed with major responsibilities, you probably don't have time to redry the dishes while taking them out of the dishwasher to be sure that every dish is spotless. Thanksgiving dinner may deserve our best effort; Saturday breakfast may call only for an adequate attempt. The annual speech to

the stockholders requires our best effort. An adequate effort may suffice for the Monday morning staff meeting.

2. *Recovering procrastinators decide that their self-esteem is not risked with every task.* So long as we feel that every task is a test of our worth, we will gift wrap the garbage. Although it is not easy, you can learn that your self-esteem is not risked on every task and live accordingly.

3. *Recovering procrastinators decide whose expectations they will try to meet, knowing that they cannot please everyone.* The belief that one is worthy only when receiving praise and approval from everyone complicates these decisions. One may want to please both boss and spouse, yet conflicting expectations make it impossible. Instead of trying the impossible, one decides to keep either the job or the spouse, especially when the ultimatum is given. Or you may receive pressure from peers to do less work and pressure from supervisors to do more work. Rather than try to please both groups, you can decide whether to retain your integrity or your friends. In order to overcome the deep need for approval that affects performance, we need a new set of beliefs about ourselves and others.

Wanda's need for approval caused her to say yes to almost every request. She would agree to collect for the Cancer Fund, and when it became obvious that she was not going to get the job done, she hired other people to do the volunteer work. Everyone knew they could count on Wanda to say yes and, in some way, get the job done.

In our procrastination study group her special project was to learn to say *no;* she needed to slow down the snowballing of her daily schedule. Just when we thought she was learning this lesson, she reported that once again she had been shot down by a charming requester. Petite, attractive Wanda agreed to guard several male prisoners while they reconditioned a building being converted into a halfway house for alcoholic women. She not only made the men party sandwiches, but she began the day by wagging her index finger at the men saying, "Don't anybody run away. Let's all stay right here."

After that incident, the group knew that Wanda needed more than general suggestions to stop the chronic yeses. The group suggested a slogan for her to use when people called to ask her to do volunteer work. "I'm sorry, but no. My time is committed for the next three months. I can't take on anything else until I complete what I'm doing."

The following week Wanda was exuberant when explaining she had turned down a request. "The lady understood," explained Wanda, "and she still likes me. It was a little scary at first, but I felt good after I did it."

Marvin chimed in, "I know what you mean. This week I said no a few times, and I liked doing it. I couldn't have done that a month ago. I was a little nervous; yet it gave me a feeling of power."

In another group Ron confessed, "I discovered that when I say no for a good reason two things happen. One, people still like me and don't get mad at me. Two, I like myself better. It's as though I'm finally taking control of my life, and I like the feeling."

People with a deep need for approval may learn by practicing more noes that most people use different criteria for approving others than what they thought. Charming procrastinators may learn that a responsible no evokes more respect and approval than an irresponsible yes.

16 STEP EIGHT: Learn How to Procrastinate Creatively

Procrastination is not always bad. It can even be helpful when used properly.

Sherie Lowe, a time-and-systems advisor and communication consultant, says:

> Procrastination is a victim, not a vice. There's nothing wrong with procrastination, as long as it doesn't hinder someone else. You need time to back up to get a head start and time to think about what you're doing. Today, in business especially, we say we should be aggressive, decisive, and know what we want to do or create. The results are instant decisions.

While some tasks and decisions require impulsiveness or routine action, others deserve creative thinking and maximum energy. This involves postponing some decisions, or planning enough in advance to allow the creative process to take place. In *The Art of Readable Writing*, Rudolf Flesch described the creative process:

> Get the facts, think hard of the best way of presenting them, and then "think aside." Let the matter drop for a while until you suddenly hit upon a combination of ideas. . . . If you don't believe that this method works for such

matters as business correspondence and reports think of all those letters you could have written twice as well had you waited until the next morning. And think of all those you did improve after you had taken time out for something else.

Creative thinking cannot be forced. Trying to force ideas is not only frustrating, it is impossible. Our minds have their own time schedule and will yield results only after sufficient incubation. Gathering and placing problems and facts in the mind well ahead of the due date fertilizes the facts with past experiences and future dreams.

This is the reason it is futile to force creativity. Switching to a different type of activity relaxes the mind's grip on that problem. While you are washing the dishes or lazily reeling in the fishing lure, the solution may break into the open and send you scurrying for pen and pad. Flesch explains, "Getting ideas out of the unconscious is the rule rather than the exception." When we wait until the last minute to do the whole job, we bypass the creative process and prophetically proclaim, "Next time I'll start earlier, because if I had had more time with this project I would have . . . ."

Waiting until ideas are clearer and more facts are available are valid concerns that are helpful to performance when we *plan* the procrastination. When we plant the problem in our minds early enough, we ward off the need for instant decision and give our minds time to test the available options. Then we feel the exhilaration of doing a creative job well.

17 STEP NINE: Use Evaluation to Grow from Experience

Driving home from the dinner party Mrs. Smith says, "It was a nice dinner party. Everyone seemed to enjoy themselves, except Joan. Did you notice how quiet she was?"

"Not really," replies Mr. Smith. "The filet was delicious, but mine was a little too rare."

We all evaluate the people and things and events that affect us.

"It was a boring meeting."

"Have you ever seen such a pretty dress?"

"You burned the bacon."

"I really enjoyed the movie."

"Your room is a disaster area."

We evaluate constantly, and successful people use evaluation to improve their skills and performance. They learn from their own experiences, and from the experiences of others.

Procrastinators, on the other hand, tend to avoid evaluation. Often their unconscious assumption is, "If I evaluate what I do, I will feel worse than if I do not. It is better not to know." This assumption is rationalized with, "I don't have time to waste on the past; I'm too busy catching up with last week's work."

Recovering procrastinators must learn to evaluate effectively what they do. Only those who know how to use

106

criticism as part of a growing process seek it, because these people view criticism as a helpful tool instead of a hurtful act. It takes positive experiences of learning from criticism and benefitting from the learning to gain this positive perspective.

In writing *Laughing and Crying with Little League,* my wife and I divided topics, wrote our respective chapters, and then exchanged chapters to criticize each other's work. When her surgical mind dissected my clever clauses, I felt cut to the quick. It was a tense process. After many such experiences of working together, we now seek each other's opinions on everything we write.

Recovering procrastinators use systematic evaluation to overcome their habit of procrastination. Effective evaluation is necessary in eliminating procrastination, because the process helps us assume responsibility for our actions and attitudes, instead of unconsciously repeating the same old behavior. Effective evaluation enables us to become the person we choose to be because it helps us to be realistic about what we can and cannot do and be and what we need to learn and to practice to improve performance and enhance self-esteem.

PRINCIPLES OF EFFECTIVE EVALUATION

1. *Effective evaluation has clear criteria for judging results and methods.* Whether or not we reach our goal of selling Mr. Robinson a carload of soap by December 31 can be evaluated simply. However, other factors need evaluation. How did Mr. Robinson talk to the salesperson? What caused Mr. Robinson to purchase the soap? Was it the salesperson's persuasive manner, or the excellent market analysis, or the advertising support promised, or the price, or the time of year?

With their tendency to see the negative, procrastinators often evaluate only the surface results. Mrs. Allen, the wife of a university dean, invited her husband's department to a Christmas dinner party. Of the 60 people invited, 48 showed up. The hostess, Mrs. Allen, was distraught. She interpreted the absences as personal rejection; it meant that the professors and their spouses did not like her. The fact that a winter storm hit the city the night before the party, knocking out telephone lines and making driving extremely hazardous, did not enter her mind. She evaluated one criterion: how many people attended the party? Forty-eight people having a good time was not appreciated because Mrs. Allen could only think of the twelve "rejections."

Effective evaluation requires more than general impressions and a single criterion. "To go with Mary to dinner at the Hilton Friday" guides John objectively; he will know if he does what he intended to do. But if the evening begins with John saying to Mary, through gritted teeth, "OK, it's Friday. Get dressed for our fun evening together," other criteria will be used to evaluate that activity.

We need criteria to evaluate not only what we plan to do, but how we do it, and the effects of the methods on people and institutions.

A simple procedure for evaluating tasks is to answer the following questions and to enlist others involved in the task to do the same.

1. What did I (we) intend to do? (State objective.)
2. What happened? (Identify action.)
3. What was helpful? Harmful?
4. What can I (we) learn from this? Are there any principles?

These simple procedures can be used to restyle one's

ways of coping with people and projects. Effective evaluation is one way procrastinators take charge of their lives.

It is recommended that procrastinators choose a simple objective, accomplish it, and practice the evaluation principles. An objective has three basic characteristics.

1. An objective describes a single action (using action verbs prevents fuzzy thinking).
2. An objective is measurable (clear criteria).
3. An objective has a time limit (deadline).

Examples of objectives:
• To finish writing the report by 4 P.M. Wednesday.
• To call on eight clients on Friday.
• To set aside 3-4 P.M. Tuesdays and Thursdays for planning time.
• To take Tommy Jr. fishing Saturday.
• To lose three pounds per week for four weeks (goal 12 pounds), starting Monday.

We may not have total control over everything we do, but we can choose an objective on which to practice our effective evaluation and learn from that process.

2. *Effective evaluation has a system of accountability.* Recovering procrastinators have found it helpful to establish their own means of accounting for their intentions and actions. They tell others what they intend to do when and then report the results to them. Knowing that they are reporting to someone motivates them to keep their word to themselves. The authority problem is absent because these people *decided* to be accountable; it is not an order from someone else. They are their own authority. Some choose spouses, others use friends, and still others enlist professional peers to be their "consciences."

Accountability in one's place of employment is often

not simple. When managers are procrastinators (and sometimes when they are not), they often refuse to clarify criteria for accountability.

Bill inherited a new supervisor. He wanted to know what was expected of him but was not told. The previous supervisor had not clarified criteria either, but everyone had tested the system until tradition was established by repetition. With the new boss everyone was nervous about expectations. If Bill worked Saturday and Sunday, was he expected to work Monday? If he worked until midnight Thursday, was he expected to be at work by 9 A.M. Wednesday? "I don't even know what kind of forms he wants when," Bill complained. Bill wanted clear criteria for accountability.

When employees are procrastinators, fuzzy criteria aid in avoiding evaluation, and accountability is seldom sought. After a few weeks in a procrastination study group, Rick decided to confront his supervisor.

"I've been working for you two years," Rick said, "and you have never once complimented me on anything I've done."

"You haven't done anything I like yet," the supervisor replied.

Mystery criteria keep employees guessing what is expected of them and put them at the whim of the employer. Lack of clear criteria encourages procrastination; when people don't know how they will be judged, the uncertainty causes them to put off doing anything that may be judged. When accountability can be established with clear, common criteria for evaluation, procrastination will decrease.

While people cannot always control the criteria by which they will be evaluated, they can establish their own criteria for evaluating performance. Your own expec-

110

tations may exceed your employer's expectations of your performance. The firm expects eight client contacts a day; you may decide twelve clients appropriate.

Not all acts warrant systematic evaluation. I do not systematically evaluate an evening with my wife; I simply enjoy her. I do not systematically evaluate the sun rising over the ocean or a late evening walk on the beach or a game with my sons. So long as routine tasks are completed satisfactorily one would not normally take time to evaluate these tasks in detail. It is enough to appreciate and savor them.

18

STEP TEN: Live Gracefully & Draw on the Power of God

The preceding chapters in Part Three have given you nine rules or principles for change, for learning how to stop procrastinating and start living. One question remains—and it is a big one: from where do we get the power to change? We may know how to change, but where does the motivation and strength to change come from?

Christians believe that the power to change comes from the gospel of Jesus Christ. We are free to change when we know and believe that God loves us unconditionally and that he daily empowers us by his Spirit. It is this faith—and not rules or principles—that enables us to overcome self-defeating patterns and to move forward into more effective ways of living. When we live by the gospel, we live grace-fully.

We have seen that procrastinators are often raised by perfectionistic parents and adopt a perfectionistic attitude toward their own lives and work. Because they do not want to fail in meeting their unrealistic standards, procrastinators put off tasks or avoid them altogether.

The gospel sets us free from this bondage to perfection. Because we know that God accepts us with all our imperfections, we are free to accept ourselves. We live by grace, each day confessing our failure to perform perfectly, and each day accepting God's forgiveness.

112

THE PROCESS OF CHANGE

While the gospel empowers us to change, we do not expect to change completely overnight. We often experience the tension between the "old person" and the new, so that we feel we are two people.

A city planner for a large Midwestern city sat in my office berating himself as he played out the scriptural drama. "I can't stand myself. It is as if there is a stranger inside me sabotaging my life."

After listening to this self-flagellation for 30 minutes I asked what specifically he failed to do that was making him feel so guilty.

"A million-dollar grant slipped through my fingers because I couldn't seem to get around to writing a final draft," he replied. "It's the story of my life—missed opportunities to do something that was worth doing. People, hundreds of people, will suffer because of me. I failed them. I failed myself. I'm so disgusted with myself. What am I going to do with that other me who keeps hurting both of us?"

The apostle Paul also felt this tension. He confessed, "I do not understand my own actions. For I do not do what I want, but I do the very thing I hate." Paul felt as though there were demonic forces inside him sabotaging his good intentions. The forces of evil caused him to fail himself and others, "Wretched man that I am . . ." was Paul's self-condemning confession.

Paul could live with his imperfection because he believed in the grace of God as revealed through Jesus the Christ. In Ephesians 2:8-9 Paul proclaims, "For by grace you have been saved through faith; and this is not your own doing, it is the gift of God—not because of works, lest any man should boast." Grace is the gift from God proclaiming that we are loved and accepted as we are.

There is nothing we can do to earn this love, because one cannot earn that which is already given. When we accept this premise about the nature and action of God, we are free from a living death. We are free from frantically fighting to prove to God and others our worth. We are free from always having to do what others tell us we ought to do or from rebelling against those who do so because we can now choose to become who we want to be instead of living the old nature that sabotages our every move and mood. By the grace of God, we choose our *oughts* and our *wants* instead of automatically accepting the claims of those out of the past and those imposed by the people in our immediate environment. Through grace the basic issue of life is solved—the acceptance of us as we are proclaims our worth. We are not loved because we are worthy, we are worthy because we are loved.

In addition to his belief in God's grace, Paul could live with his imperfection because he believed in people's ability to change. Throughout his writings Paul urges us to choose a more "perfect" way, which assumes our ability to grow in the spirit of Christ. We gradually learn the new way of living in the spirit of love and are then committed to trying to eliminate harmful old habits and to developing new ways of doing what we believe.

By grace we are free from attending church, serving charitable causes, and trying to change unjust social and political systems because we *ought to* or are *afraid not to*. When at our best, we perform these services because it is in our new nature to do so. Ideally, we gradually grow from a predominant "ought to" life to a "want to" way of being. We do deeds not to be "perfect" or even to be praised or liked, but to express something inside ourselves. We grow from always trying to prove our worth to expressing our gratitude to God and others.

While gradually changing, we learn to live in the spirit of Christ. By the grace of God and the help of friends and family, the gap between our intentions and actions gradually narrows. Though we will not reach perfection, we can enjoy life as we learn and laugh, grope and grow, confront and care and work and play with others, by the grace of God.

19 Overcoming Procrastination in Organizations

According to Robert Half, Inc. of New York, the most damaging crime against business is time theft. "While kickbacks, employee pilferage, arson, insurance fraud, shoplifting, embezzlement and other recognized crimes amount to between 30 and 40 billion dollars a year, time theft—the deliberate waste and misuse of on-the-job time will cost American economy at $80 billion [in 1978]." Procrastination is expensive, whether the organization is religious, civic, educational, business, or any group of people trying to accomplish something. The following principles are suggested to help diminish procrastination in organizations.

1. *When people know why they do what they do, they procrastinate less.* When people do not know why they do what they do, they get bored. Achievement-motivated people need a reason to work eight, ten, or fourteen hours a day, and money is not a sufficient reason for most people. Every job should fit some place in the system which helps an organization fulfill its purpose.

2. *When people know what is expected of them, the temptation to procrastinate is lessened.* When people do not know what they are expected to do and how they are expected to act and how they will be evaluated, they avoid completing tasks. Without clear criteria, people get

116

frustrated and confused and procrastinate to avoid the unknown.

3. *When people are permitted to be responsible for their work, they procrastinate less.* A boss who can't or won't delegate responsibility can anticipate employees procrastinating. When the boss has to examine every piece of work, participate in every big and little decision, and place the royal seal of acceptability on everything, employees begin feeling and acting like irresponsible children. Knowing that their reports, or letters, or projects will be reworked, employees lose a sense of responsibility and power and self-esteem and adjust to doing half a job.

Employers will decrease the procrastination of employees if they refuse to "nag," reminding employees of what they are supposed to do. If I know you will tell me when I *have* to do something, I can forget it until the third memo.

Employers can expect work on time. Edwin Bliss suggests, "If you ask people to do things and they usually don't get around to them, stop asking yourself, 'What's the matter with people these days?' Instead, ask yourself 'What is the matter with *me?* What am I doing (or failing to do) that causes people to give empty promises?' "

Finally, employers can refuse to rescue people. Playing organizational lifeguard, saving people who cannot get around to doing their work, enhances the employer's self-esteem while diminishing the confidence of the one being saved. If we know that someone else will do the job if we don't, we can twiddle our thumbs until the rescuer appears either to do the job or assign it to someone else.

4. *When evaluation is a regular process for improving performance, procrastination is lessened.* When people

are evaluated only when problems arise, they avoid the boss as much as possible, and avoid getting work completed because of the possible condemnation. When evaluation is viewed as a way of keeping an employee in line rather than a natural process for improving performance, procrastination is a natural response.

5. *When workers are adequately challenged, procrastination is lessened.* Too much to do frustrates people, defeats their need to do their best, and forces them to administer by impulse. But too little to do also affects self-esteem and job satisfaction, and it lures people into learning how to procrastinate. Achievement-motivated people do not like this lack of challenge, but with enough practice they adjust to it.

6. *Setting clear deadlines diminishes procrastination.* A supervisor called an employee into the office and asked him for an overdue report.

"It isn't ready," the employee said.

"I told you to get that report ready two weeks ago. Why isn't it ready?"

"You didn't tell me *when* it had to be ready."

Without a *when* most people let the task get lost in the confusion of competing causes. We need deadlines to set priorities and plan our work.

7. *The more people are involved in deciding what they do the less they procrastinate.* Orders from on high usually meet resistance from below—and usually with procrastination. Involving people in the decisions that affect their working conditions lessens the tendency to procrastinate.

Effective management creates working conditions in which people are encouraged to be responsible first to themselves and then to others for their performance and product. When people's self-esteem is high, their sense of power is intact, and their work planned, then their energy, creativity, and presence makes a positive difference in the organization.

Appendix   How to Use This Book in a Procrastination Group

Many people have found that sharing problems of procrastination, either as a procrastinator or as a victim of a procrastinator, is helpful. Realizing that others act and feel the same way relieves some of the tension procrastinators feel, and by sharing problems, the members support each other in their efforts to change.

BASIC FEATURES OF THE PROCRASTINATION GROUP

Size. The group should be small enough for each person to share thoughts and feelings at every meeting. If the group is larger than 20 people, it could be broken into subgroups for most of the meeting time.

Time. The meeting needs to last at least 90 minutes, for people need time to consider content, exchange ideas, and work on personal agenda with others. It usually takes 30 minutes after people's bodies arrive for their emotions to catch up. Because the subject is uncomfortable and embarrassing for many, especially during the first few sessions, it takes time for them to relax enough to verbalize their problems.

Frequency of Meeting. Once a week is recommended. During the study people will try to change their lives,

120

and while struggling they need support, encouragement, and specific suggestions. Two weeks of "failure" without any support or encouragement can cause people to give up. The groups for the court-assigned people mentioned in Chapter 1 met four consecutive days, two hours per day, and were urged to use the partner plan as a support system.

Contract Participation. Contract with members to give the study group top priority in their schedules. To be effective the contract should include attendance at every meeting, unless the person is ill or a serious emergency arises. People who cannot attend every meeting should not attend the group. For the study to be helpful it has to have top priority. The contract should include the number of meetings—four, eight, ten, or twelve. People will agree to a specific number of meetings, but are reluctant to enter an open-ended contract. Being on time should be part of the contract. Procrastinators are often late to meetings and for appointments. In addition to needing the time to work on problems, this principle directly calls for a change in behavior.

Nature of Participation. Each person will be expected to share ideas, feelings, and personal experiences. No one should be *pressured* to confess anything, but everyone will be expected to share enough to help themselves and others. A level of trust must be established for participants to work with each other.

Physical Facilities. The meeting place should be comfortable and arranged informally. A lectern facing chairs in a row evokes antiauthority feelings and suggests that a teacher or parent will solve one's problems. If possible, arrange the room or setting where everyone can see everyone else.

Here are some procedures that have been helpful with groups. Three meetings are described to give a flow of the activities.

FIRST MEETING

1. Begin each meeting with an activity that helps everyone speak. Use this procedure as a get-acquainted period. In one group for the first four meetings we began by telling our names and "confessing" such things as "My favorite dessert is . . ."; "My hobbies are . . ."; and "My favorite television program is . . . ." This served two functions. If affirmed our right to talk about ourselves, and it gave everyone a chance to get used to speaking in the group.

2. Ask each person to write what he or she expects from the study group. Expectations should be as specific as possible.

3. Ask participants to form a subgroup with two or three other people, share their expectations, and then collate their group's expectations on newsprint.

4. Ask representatives from each group to share their group's expectations with the total group.

5. Write all the expectations on another piece of newsprint to declare the group agenda.

6. Ask for additional suggestions.

7. General discussion and acceptance of agenda concludes the working. If the process works well (which it does when people are encouraged to participate), participants think and feel that their needs will be met to some degree and that they have ownership in the group.

8. Ask each participant to tell in one or two words how he or she *feels* about the meeting. This helps participants practice evaluating and giving feedback, two skills many will need to learn. Each meeting should be evalu-

ated to demonstrate that it is acceptable for people to experience and respond differently to the same stimulus.

9. Assign participants a value-clarification exercise which they are to bring to the next meeting. (Weekly assignments assist in practicing meeting deadlines.) It is helpful to have a simple form available.

Name _____

The Ten Most Important Things in My Life Are:
1.
2.
3.
4.
5.
6.
7.
8.
9.
10.

SECOND MEETING

1. After the get-acquainted period, form subgroups and share the values recorded on the form.

2. Evaluate the exercise in the total group. Ask each person to tell his or her experience of writing the values and talking about them with others.

3. The leader describes the characteristics of procrastinators and illustrates the content by confessing how he or she is affected by the problem. The leader sets the tone of the group and the level of trust is set by his or her confessions.

4. Ask participants how they are affected by procrastination. "Is this true to your experience?" "Does it sound familiar?" All people may not participate at this point be-

cause of their uncomfortableness with the problems and people. Form groups of three or four to discuss their personal experiences.

5. After a general discussion, which may lead to someone asking for specific help with a specific problem, evaluate the meeting. Incidentally, the leader needs to keep in mind that the participants are experts on this subject and will have many ideas that will be helpful to others.

6. Use this form to have participants work on goal setting in preparation for the next meeting:

Name _____
List your goals for:
   One year
   Two years
   Five years
   Ten years

According to group participants, writing their goals was the most helpful activity of study. I repeat this here because it is tempting to eliminate it.

THIRD MEETING

1. After the get-acquainted activity, form subgroups to share personal goals.

2. Evaluate the goals exercise in the total group. "Did you have trouble writing your goals?" "Was the exercise helpful?" "How did you feel telling others about your goals and listening to them describe theirs?"

3. Introduce the causes of procrastination and adjust exercises as necessary.

4. Evaluate.

5. Assign a portion of this book to be discussed in the next meeting.

The preceding is sufficient to give an idea of the flow

of a study group. It would be helpful for each member to read this book. With this background, sections of the book could be assigned each week and group exercises and discussions could be designed to illustrate the material.

By at least the third session people will be comfortable enough to share their specific problems with procrastination. Participants will suggest solutions to each other, and when there is a victory, cheers will abound. When failure is reported, specific feedback can be given. By the fourth week participants probably will be dealing with everything from sloppy spouses to teacher-student relations, from customer complaints to procrastinating bosses.

The bonus of a procrastination study group is the friendships that are formed while trying to change the ways one relates to people and projects.

Books for Further Study

Battista, O. A. *How to Enjoy Work and Get More Fun Out of Life.* Englewood Cliffs, N.J.: Prentice-Hall, Inc., 1957.

Bliss, Edwin C. *Getting Things Done: The ABC's of Time Management.* New York: Charles Scribner's Sons, 1976.

Dayton, Edward R. *Tools for Time Management.* Grand Rapids: Zondervan, 1974.

Drucker, Peter F. *The Effective Executive.* New York: Harper & Row, 1967.

Fanning, Tony and Robbie. *Get It All Done and Still Be Human.* Radnor, Pa.: Chilton Book Co., 1979.

Lakein, Allan. *How to Get Control of Your Time and Your Life.* New York: New American Library, 1974.

LeBoeuf, Michael. *Working Smart: How to Accomplish More in Half the Time.* New York: Warner Books, 1980.

Leas, Speed B. *Time Management.* Nashville: Abingdon Press, 1978.

Love, Sydney F. *Mastery and Management of Time.* Englewood Cliffs, N.J.: Prentice-Hall, Inc., 1978.

Mackinzie, R. Alec. *The Time Trap: How to Get More Done in Less Time.* New York: McGraw-Hill Book Company, 1975.

Mackinzie, Alec, and Waldo, Kay Cronkite. *About Time: A Woman's Guide to Time Management.* New York: McGraw-Hill, 1981.

Moskowitz, Robert. *How to Organize Your Work and Your Life.* Doubleday, 1981.

Reynolds, Helen, and Tramel, Mary E. *Executive Time Management.* Englewood Cliffs, N.J.: Prentice-Hall, 1979.

Winston, Stephanie. *Getting Organized: The Easy Way to Put Your Life in Order.* New York: W. W. Norton, 1978.